CREATIVE
HOMEOWNER®

DESIGN IDEAS for
Bathrooms

CREATIVE HOMEOWNER®, Upper Saddle River, New Jersey

DESIGN IDEAS FOR BATHROOMS, SECOND EDITION

SENIOR EDITOR	Kathie Robitz
GRAPHIC DESIGNER	Kathryn Wityk
PHOTO COORDINATOR	Mary Dolan
JUNIOR EDITOR	Jennifer Calvert
DIGITAL IMAGING SPECIALIST	Frank Dyer
INDEXER	Schroeder Indexing Services
DESIGN IDEAS COVER CONCEPT	Glee Barre
COVER DESIGN	Kathryn Wityk
FRONT COVER PHOTOGRAPHY	(main) Eric Roth, design: www.svdesign.com (top right) Eric Roth, architect: Eck MacNeely Architects (center right) Eric Roth, design: www.warnercunningham.com (bottom left) Mark Samu, courtesy of Hearst Magazines (bottom center) courtesy of Sonoma (bottom right) Eric Roth, design: Tile Showcase
BACK COVER PHOTOGRAPHY	(top) Bob Greenspan, stylist: Susan Andrews (bottom) Mark Samu, design: Kollath-McCann Design

CREATIVE HOMEOWNER

VICE PRESIDENT AND PUBLISHER	Timothy O. Bakke
MANAGING EDITOR	Fran J. Donegan
ART DIRECTOR	David Geer
PRODUCTION COORDINATOR	Sara M. Markowitz

Current Printing (last digit)
10 9 8 7 6 5 4 3 2

Design Ideas for Bathrooms, Second Edition
Library of Congress Control Number: 2008934562
ISBN-10: 1-58011-437-7
ISBN-13: 978-1-58011-437-0

Manufactured in the United States of America

CREATIVE HOMEOWNER®
A Division of Federal Marketing Corp.
24 Park Way
Upper Saddle River, NJ 07458
www.creativehomeowner.com

Dedication

To my father, Vilas J. Boyle, who got me started.

Contents

Bathrooms are complex spaces, made up of many elements that must work together smoothly to ensure comfort, convenience, and safety. And now this once strictly utilitarian space has become a "designer" room. You'll want every bath in your house to be beautiful, especially the master bathroom. This will be your serene retreat from daily life, filled with as many amenities as your budget allows.

Introduction

If you have bought *Design Ideas for Bathrooms*, Second Edition, you are embarking on some kind of bathroom project—or at least thinking about it. It may be a simple facelift, a major remodeling, or the construction of an entirely new space. Whatever your goal, you'll be grateful that you have found this guide through the dizzying world of trends and the staggering number of available products. The pages that follow will introduce you to all of the elements you must consider—fixtures, fittings, surface materials, cabinets, lighting, and ventilation systems. The information, tips, and bright ideas supplied will help you plan your project and decide which products best meet your needs, taste, and budget. You're sure to find the inspiration you need to make your design dreams become reality.

LEFT Natural materials enhance a back-to-nature design philosophy.

TOP Style-specific products, such as the Mediterranean-inspired lamps and tile, help to establish a mood.

ABOVE Combining a variety of materials, such as stone, glass, and metal adds visual excitement.

Starting Points

Unless you are older than 30—or live in a house that is 40 years old or older—you may not remember how boring and dysfunctional bathrooms used to be. Once cramped and inefficient, older baths generally contained an unimaginative arrangement of toilet, sink, tub, and maybe a shower; yet in the typical one-bath house of the time, they had to serve the whole family. Happily, the boring bath is a thing of the past. Today's baths are functional and good-looking, and often equipped with luxurious health-club amenities. Here are a few ideas for a new or revitalized bath of your own.

- **designed for <u>you</u>**
- **formulate ideas**
- **work with space**
- **master baths**
- **family baths**
- **half-baths**
- **universal design**

A view of the hillside and plenty of natural light is conducive to relaxation in this master bath. The simple forms and materials are in keeping with the room's low-key mood.

LEFT Just off the bathing area, two lavs and a dressing table provide a space for grooming that is separate from the rest of the room.

BELOW LEFT A bay accommodates the built-in whirlpool tub. The position of the windows above the tub, rather than level with it, improves privacy.

BELOW RIGHT You can see in this photo how the floor plan was designed to remain open and yet conducive to compartmentalized areas.

OPPOSITE BOTTOM A large walk-in shower benefits from natural light thanks to a glass-block window. The glass shower door allows that light to filter into the room.

OPPOSITE TOP Clever linen storage and a built-in hamper have been tucked conveniently between the wall studs, leaving extra room for the vanity area.

devise a floor plan that complements your lifestyle

today's home probably contains a couple of bathrooms, maybe more—a powder room conveniently located near activity areas, a bath just for kids or especially for guests, and of course, the queen of them all, the master bath. In many cases, it is also a designer room, with decorating schemes that reflect personal tastes and with equipment that suits individual needs and the desire for pampering. Do you dream of a luxurious soak at the end of the day? Whatever your budget or space situation, there is a tub to make that fantasy come true. If you prefer showering, your choices are also varied, from a compact corner unit to a spacious spa-like stall with steam capability. It's the same story with sinks, toilets, and faucets—they all range from serviceable to sybaritic, and from cost-conscious to pricey.

designed for you

When it comes to the look of the bath, you can get really personal. Fixtures, fittings, surfacing materials, and accessories—available in many sizes, shapes, colors, and styles—let you easily create whatever look you like. Go sleek and contemporary, or cozy and traditional, in the master bath; or create a Victorian look with vintage-style fixtures. You can let yourself go in a kids' bath with whimsical faucets, colorful tiles, and playful accessories that make the room cheerful and appealing. And a powder room is the perfect place for drama and glamour. Skylights over the tub, a window in the shower, and access to a private garden or patio are other ways to personalize.

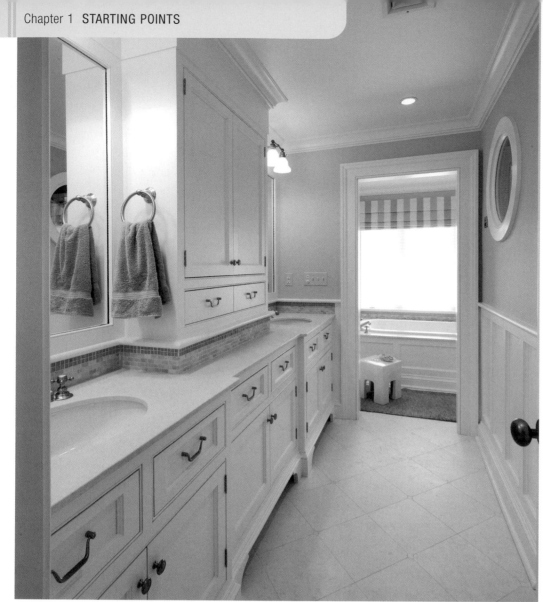

ABOVE LEFT This long corridor, outfitted with two lavs and plenty of built-in storage, leads to a separate room that houses the tub and walk-in shower.

ABOVE RIGHT The oculus permits a view into the grooming area from the shower and breaks up a long wall with an interesting architectural detail.

LEFT A detail of the tub surround offers a glimpse at the pretty band of tile that has been used as a backsplash. The same treatment appears behind the vanity counter.

OPPOSITE TOP In another, more compact shared space, a custom vanity features his and her grooming stations.

OPPOSITE BOTTOM A glass enclosure defines the room's shower while a half-wall next to the tub conceals the toilet.

what each design pro knows

- **Architects** plan, design, and oversee new construction and major remodels. You will need one if your project involves an addition or an extensive makeover of existing space.
- **Certified Bath Designers (CBD)** are schooled in all aspects of bathroom design, from layouts, to equipment and materials, to wiring and plumbing. Before choosing one, make sure your design sensibilities mesh.
- **Interior designers** work to create a functional and aesthetically pleasing interior. They may provide floor plans and renderings; plan lighting; advise about color; assist in the selection and purchase of materials, products, and fixtures; and monitor installation.
- **General contractors** usually work from plans drawn up by other professionals. They will get permits, install cabinets, and oversee the work of the electrician and other trades. Some specialize in bathrooms, and some work in partnership with designers.

wash 'n wear

Marble can be damaged by corrosive products. Ask your marble dealer to recommend a gentle way to remove soap scum and other stains.

how to relax

Consider a custom steam shower or a freestanding unit with all of the trimmings. If adding such luxury will put your budget over the top, consider a steam unit for a tub-and-shower combination or an economical steam generator for your existing shower stall.

ABOVE An elliptical bathtub, sculpted from solid marble, has a look of lightness and grace. It stands here almost as a piece of modern art.

BELOW The simplicity of the cabinetry and lighting provides a quiet backdrop for the elegant stone walls and fixtures.

OPPOSITE Organic white-cotton towels that have been rolled tightly are neatly displayed in an open under-counter storage compartment.

today's bathrooms are variously described as beautiful, luxurious, relaxing, and even romantic. But let's not forget functional. The bath is a hard-working and complex room and must be planned with careful attention to such practical matters as layout, safety, storage, durability, and maintenance. Sure, picking out fixtures, finishes, and colors is fun. But before you start shopping, think about some basics—what kind of bath are you planning? Who will use it? What features will it include? How much space is available? How much can you spend? To keep costs manageable, make use of existing space somewhere in your house if you can. Adding on could put you over budget.

formulate ideas

Once you have established the basics, draw up a wish list; then pare it down as space and budget dictate. Paging through design books, home-improvement magazines, and catalogs, and visiting home centers and showrooms will give you an idea of the fixtures and fittings available in your price range. Think about storage, too. If possible, aim for a variety of storage units—base cabinets with several drawer sizes, open shelves, tall cupboards for linens. Finishing materials are also important. Choose durable, moisture-resistant, and easy-to-clean surfaces. Last but not least, ensure safety with good lighting and adequate ventilation to prevent the buildup of mold or mildew.

look of luxe
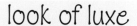

It's hard to beat the upscale look that stone adds to a bathroom. But a more practical choice for the floor may be a ceramic tile look-alike.

OPPOSITE TOP Custom storage built into the wall and a wall-mounted toilet frees floor space in tight quarters.

LEFT AND FAR LEFT Creative space planning allowed the owners of this house to add a full bath to their recently finished attic by overcoming a steeply pitched roofline.

and work out details

LEFT A combination of handsome, hardworking materials, such as ceramic tile and stone, will hold up well in a room that gets lots of use.

RIGHT Extending moisture-resistant ceramic tile to the ceiling just above the shower is a practical choice, even in a well-ventilated space.

points of view

Bathroom layouts are as varied today as those of kitchens. Here are a few floor plans you might consider for your project.

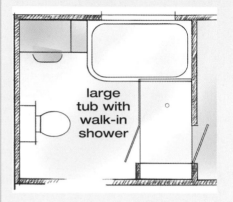

large tub with walk-in shower

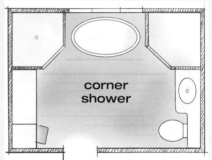

corner shower

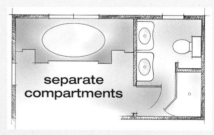

separate compartments

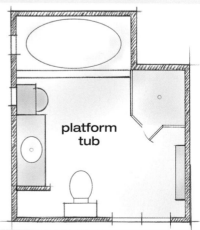

platform tub

ABOVE Even if you have limited space that precludes separate bathing, grooming, and toileting areas, arrange fixtures and cabinetry to visually compartmentalize the room. An example is this tall cabinet that hides the toilet.

OPPOSITE Half-walls are an excellent way to divide space without closing off one part of a room from natural light.

work with space

is space tight in your new or remodeled bath? Try some simple, space-stretching strategies to make it look and feel larger. Small-scale fixtures, for example, are as functional as their full-size cousins but save significant amounts of space. Excellent examples are sinks and toilets that are designed to fit into a small corner. Natural light is a great space-expander, too—if possible, add a skylight or enlarge existing windows. Then resist the impulse to hang fussy curtains. Leave the windows unadorned, or put up simple blinds if privacy is an issue. A white or pale color scheme, even on the floor, will also make the room look bigger, as will large expanses of mirror. Finally, create the illusion of greater floor space by ditching the vanity in favor of a pedestal or console-style sink. On the other hand, if the space is awkward or oddly shaped, look for ways to work with it. Make use of knee walls by building storage into them, or tuck the toilet or tub under an eave.

RIGHT Tile and glass walls form an enclosure for this unusual custom shower. Its corner location makes good use of space.

BELOW The shower's half-solid wall picks up on the tiled wainscot that runs throughout the room.

Go Green

Install water-efficient faucets and toilets. Look for ones that are endorsed by the EPA with a WaterSense label.

BELOW Again, a half-wall acts as a partition. In this modest-size bathroom, it delineates the toileting and showering areas without completely closing them off from the rest of the room.

personalize the layout

divide and conquer

A shared bath works best as a series of separate compartments—a water closet for the toilet, a free-standing shower, a tub alcove, and self-contained sinks. Providing these islands of privacy and preventing traffic jams is easier in a large room, but clever placement of fixtures or the addition of short walls or partitions can divide and conquer modest dimensions, too.

ABOVE A large vanity wall divides this spacious layout. The shower can be entered at the far end of the wall, while the bath is located behind the wall at the end in the foreground.

LEFT Frosted-glass partitions offer privacy while maintaining the clean lines of this design.

RIGHT The ultimate privacy is a completely separate toileting room. When space is as tight as it is here, a pocket door solves the problem.

BELOW LEFT Opening up the ceiling to the rafters adds rustic charm to this design, and the additional height makes the small space feel larger.

BELOW RIGHT Maintaining an all-neutral scheme visually opens up the space here. Even the partition separating the vanity from the toilet is unobtrusive.

double the sum

A large vanity cabinet will take up more floor space in a bathroom, but it provides a lot of storage.

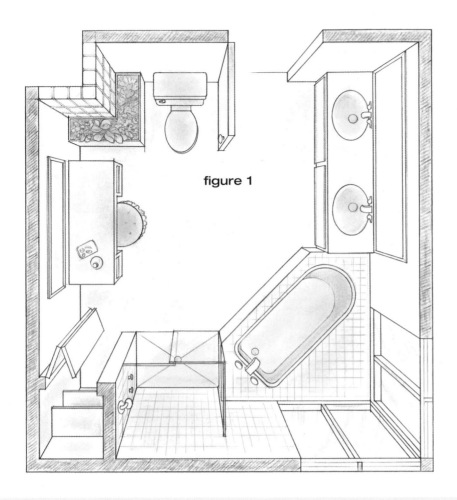

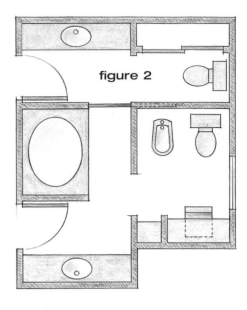

FIGURE ONE An angled bathtub conserves floor space and allows for a double vanity.

FIGURE TWO An adjacent half-bath boosts a master bath's use.

the master bathroom: how suite it is

FIGURE THREE A grand layout provides two separate but connected bathrooms within a large master suite.

FIGURE FOUR His and her zones open via pocket doors to a shared tub.

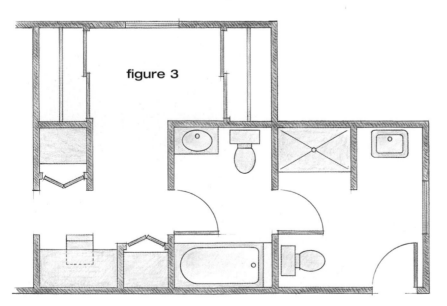

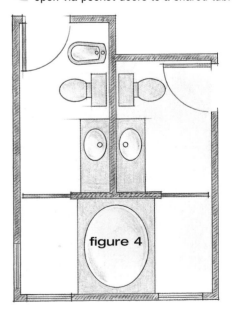

Often sequestered in a corner or wing of the house, today's master bath is part of an entire suite, an ensemble of rooms that includes a bedroom, dressing area, perhaps a sitting area, and sometimes even a deck, balcony, or private garden. But what if you don't happen to have a wing to spare? Must you give up the dream of an at-home sanctuary where you can escape the hubbub of the household and unwind from the tensions of the workday? You can build an addition to your house, of course, but this is the most expensive way to go and may put you over budget. Before you commit to that course, look around for existing usable space that can be converted into a bigger and better bath, keeping in mind that even a few square feet can make an important difference. For example, you may be able to expand a bath that adjoins your current bedroom by borrowing space from a bedroom or nearby hall closet, or the hall itself. If you have a big bedroom, you might consider sacrificing some of its square footage to enlarge the bath. Another idea—transform part, or all, of an adjacent and seldom-used bedroom into a master bath. This approach would work especially well for empty-nesters with room to spare. And don't overlook the possibility of annexing the attic—with a little imaginative remodeling, it could become the new and luxuriously private master suite you have always wanted.

master baths

BELOW LEFT Special touches, such as the custom cabinetry and an over-size walk-in shower, are highly desirable master-bath amenities.

BELOW The whirlpool tub's spacious granite deck and wood-paneled skirt and the matching cabinet are more examples of value-added details.

ABOVE LEFT Steps away from the tub area, custom cabinetry topped with dark, rich marble creates a vanity with separate his and her lavs.

ABOVE All set for a sybaritic soak? This deep tub is clearly the focal point in the design. Translucent shades filter the light without compromising privacy.

LEFT Multiple jets provide relief to sore muscles from every direction.

OPPOSITE LEFT The large walk-in shower has fixed showerheads, including a large rain shower.

OPPOSITE RIGHT A "washlet" toilet with a built-in personal-cleansing system features a sleek modern design.

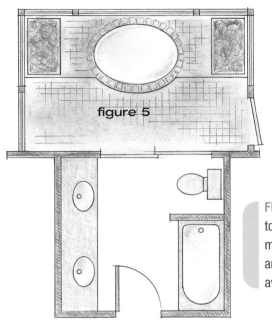

figure 5

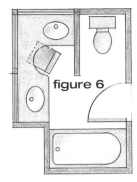

figure 6

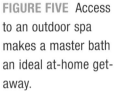

FIGURE SIX An L-shaped countertop can make way for a pair of sinks as well as a dressing table.

FIGURE SEVEN A separate grooming area is a better use of shared space.

FIGURE FIVE Access to an outdoor spa makes a master bath an ideal at-home getaway.

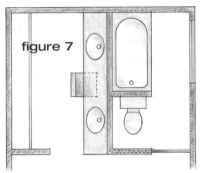

figure 7

top of the line materials and finishes

beat bathroom gridlock with a multitask layout

family baths

unlike master suites, which are used by only one or two people, family baths may have to service adults, children, and senior citizens; and they require a plan that is flexible and convenient for everyone. To prevent long lines from forming outside the bathroom door on busy mornings, arrange the room for simultaneous use by more than one person with at least a modicum of privacy. For example, use some of the space to create a private toilet compartment; then place the tub and shower in one part of the room and vanity in another, allowing one person to brush her teeth while another is showering. Circumvent clutter by building in plenty of storage—cabinets, open shelves, and robe and towel hooks will help stow everybody's stuff.

ABOVE LEFT The walk-in shower has a hand-held showerhead that can be used by everyone, from the shortest to the tallest family member.

ABOVE RIGHT A super-size vanity and plenty of storage can accommodate everyone's needs.

OPPOSITE TOP Personalized towels, a funky shower curtain, and perhaps a few accessories can turn any bathroom into one that's reserved for the kids.

neat nooks

Designed to accommodate large bath towels, these storage cubbies put every square inch to work in this kid's bathroom.

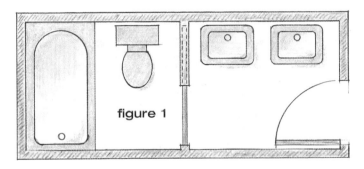

FIGURE ONE Locating the sinks, which are the most-used fixtures, nearest the door is logical.

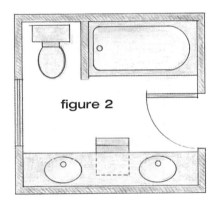

FIGURE TWO A partition next to the toilet expands the use of a bathroom without a costly addition.

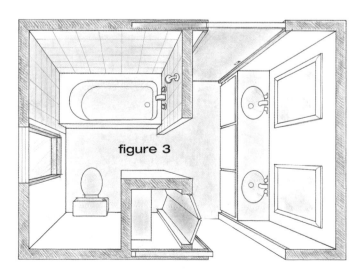

FIGURE THREE Pocket doors, installed around this room, do not use up floor space, allowing an improved floor plan.

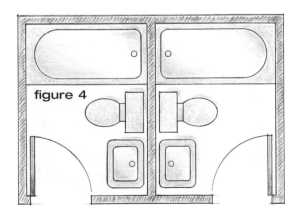

FIGURE FOUR Back-to-back plumbing creates two smaller bathrooms from one formerly large space.

furnished with only a sink and toilet, half-baths are handy little spaces. Used as powder rooms for the convenience of guests, they are typically placed on the first floor near public areas. If possible, create a sense of privacy for your guests by positioning a powder room so that it does not open immediately onto a living room, dining room, family room, or wherever people will congregate in your household. Find a spot in the front hall or around the corner from activity areas.

Although guests generally don't linger in powder rooms, these diminutive spaces do get a lot of use, especially if you entertain often. Don't skimp on quality; instead, invest in fixtures that can be counted on to work efficiently over time. If space is especially tight, investigate small-scale fixtures. A pedestal sink consumes less floor area than a sink-vanity combination; but to compensate for the loss of a vanity counter, install a shelf to hold soaps and guests' makeup paraphernalia. Be sure to include a mirror with lighting.

Other likely places for a half-bath are near a guest bedroom, in a finished basement, off the kitchen, or in the bedroom wing to supplement a family bath.

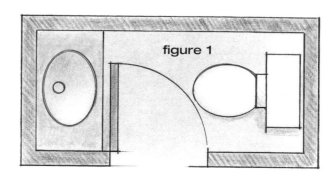

half-baths

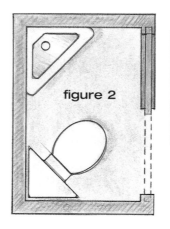

FIGURE ONE In a long, narrow room, place the toilet and the sink on opposite walls.

FIGURE TWO Corner fixtures and a pocket door are small-space solutions.

add comfort, style, and value with this amenity

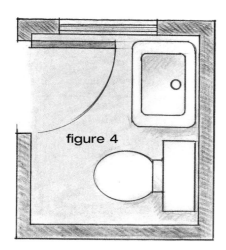

FIGURE FOUR Locate the sink and the toilet on the same wall to conserve floor space.

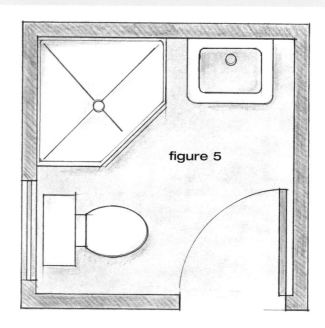

FIGURE FIVE A corner shower unit can convert a half-bath into a three-quarter bath.

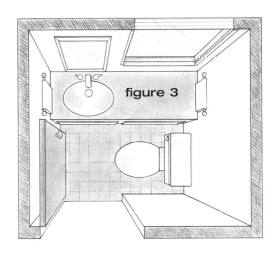

FIGURE THREE A large vanity is helpful if a half-bath doubles as an extra grooming area on busy mornings.

LEFT Even the addition of a small powder room can increase a home's value, especially if it's outfitted with attractive lighting, a nice vanity or lav, and a pretty mirror.

ABOVE Including a shower can turn a half-bath into a three-quarter bath. Some people prefer it to a full-size bathroom, but if it's the only one in the house, include a tub for resale value.

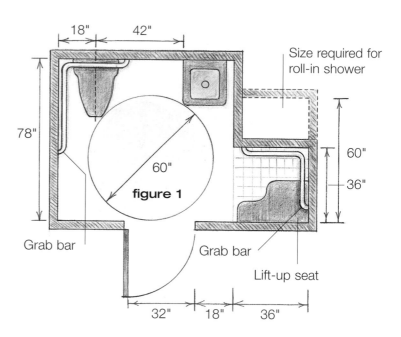

FIGURE ONE Two types of showers are geared for wheelchair use. People who can leave the wheelchair can move onto the seat of a small shower. If the person must remain in the wheelchair while bathing, a roll-in shower must be installed (indicated by dashed lines).

plan the space to be safe and comfortable for all

a few decades ago, bathroom designers and product manufacturers awoke to the fact that bathrooms need to be not only safe for all members of the family but also accessible for all people, of all levels of physical abilities. The result was Universal Design, which assures safety, convenience, and maneuverability for anyone who uses the bath.

universal design

To accommodate people with limited mobility or poor eyesight, designers suggest placing grab bars strategically—around the tub, toilet, and shower—installing lever-style faucets, and making sure lights are bright in every corner of the room, particularly the shower. Swing-open doors present problems for wheelchair users. Make access easier by replacing a conventional door with a pocket door; if space permits, allow enough of an area in the center of the room for a wheelchair to turn around. Some manufacturers produce bathtubs and sinks that cater to wheelchair users, and showers with built-in seats are also available. Install a flat-threshold shower compartment that won't obstruct entry by a wheelchair.

While you're planning your new bath, why not incorporate some ease-of-use features that you might appreciate in the future if not now? Consider easy-grip C-shaped cabinet hardware, nonslip floors or mats in the tub and shower, and scald-protection faucets. A light switch outside the bathroom door might also be helpful.

hold on

Grab bars in bathtubs and showers are helpful for people of any age or physical ability.

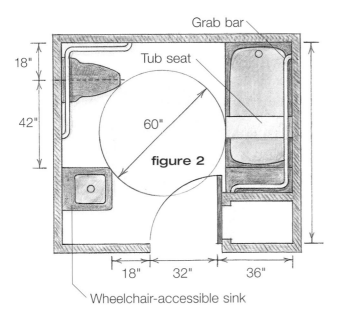

Grab bar

Tub seat

18"

42"

60"

figure 2

18"   32"   36"

Wheelchair-accessible sink

FIGURE TWO These are the minimum clearances and accessories required for wheelchair access in a bathroom with a tub. The 60-in. clear circle allows a person in a wheelchair to turn around.

LEFT A grab bar must be securely anchored to the wall or the tub deck. Today's styles include finishes to match the room's other hardware or fittings.

ABOVE Sinks should be installed at a comfortable height for the people who will use them. Wrist-blade handles, as seen here, are the easiest to use for both the youngest and oldest family members.

2

Bath and Shower Power

The refreshing and restorative qualities of water are powerful, whether we soak in it or stand under streams of it. And when it's time to equip your bathroom, you'll find that many types of "water experiences" are available. Are you typically in a hurry to get on with your day? Then you may be happy with a no-frills tub or shower. But if you've got the time or the desire for some relaxation, you'll be interested in today's pampering soaking tubs, spa-like whirlpools, and fully loaded showers. Here, we have gathered all types of bathing options, from simple to sumptuous, for your consideration.

- **bathtubs**
- **showers**
- **fittings**

You've got options! Suit yourself with a lingering soak, a pulsating massage, or a refreshing rain shower.

dress for success

Fabric shades that are easy to adjust are a smart idea. But make sure they are treated to resist moisture.

bathtubs

Sizes, shapes, and features vary, but there are only a few basic types of bathtubs in terms of installation. Placed against walls on three sides, alcove, or recessed tubs are the most common. Freestanding tubs may have feet, legs, or a pedestal; some may sit directly on the floor. Drop-in tubs are installed inside a platform or a finished surround.

The most common tub materials include fiberglass, which is lightweight and inexpensive but shows scratches and other types of wear. High-quality acrylic is lightweight, too—essential if you're selecting an extra-large tub—but more durable. Fiberglass and acrylic can be molded into different shapes. Porcelain or enamel over cast iron is almost indestuctible, but it's heavy. Porcelain or enamel over steel is fairly lightweight, but it can chip and rust. Less common examples include sophisticated—and demanding—copper, stainless steel, teak, concrete, and stone.

OPPOSITE TOP LEFT Modern materials update a standard tub.

OPPOSITE TOP RIGHT A deep, round soaking tub benefits from a circular skylight that mirrors its shape.

OPPOSITE BOTTOM This custom-tiled tub surround is linked visually with the shower.

ABOVE RIGHT Modeled after a French "bateau tub," this reproduction has a porcelain enamel interior and a copper exterior.

RIGHT You can soak in style in this oversize vessel.

shopping for a tub

How much can you spend? How much space do you have? A one-piece tub and shower unit can cost as little as $300; a tub with fancy spa features can set you back several thousand dollars or more. You can save a bundle by selecting only those features you really want—and will use.

Five-ft.-long alcove tubs or corner models work well in small spaces; freestanding tubs and large whirlpools may be as much as 7 ft. long and 5 ft. wide. If you're remodeling, size matters: some models may not fit through existing doors and hallways. Weight is important, too. Large tubs filled with lots of water may need additional floor support.

The bottom line is buy the best tub you can afford. Test it in the showroom. Make sure that it's comfortable and that you can get in and out of it easily.

LEFT A double-size whirlpool tub set into a platform looks dramatic, but the steps could pose a safety hazard for wet feet.

BELOW This freestanding tub keeps the bathroom airy and open because it doesn't require a boxy surround or deck.

pamper yourself with a custom bathing experience

OPPOSITE TOP A free-standing tub can be extra deep and wide, so check the available floor space.

OPPOSITE BOTTOM LEFT A hand-carved tub is one-of-a-kind.

OPPOSITE BOTTOM RIGHT A Roman bath inspired this design, but stone tubs come in many styles.

bathtub safety

With its potentially slippery surfaces and unforgiving materials, your beautiful new bathroom can be a hazardous place. However, you can prevent mishaps.

- Buy a tub with a nonslip, textured bottom.
- Select a tub that you can get into and out of easily, and that has controls or fixtures in an accessible location.
- Be aware that step-up platforms may be risky. Experts recommend no more than one step, which should be less than 7 in. high and at least 10 in. deep.
- Place solidly anchored grab bars with textured, easy-grip surfaces in a couple of strategic places on the tub wall or deck.
- Choose antiscald faucets with easy-turn lever-style handles.
- Use ground-fault circuit interrupters (GFCI) on outlets and moisture-proof fixtures near the tub.

ABOVE Fabricated by hand in stainless steel, this Japanese soaking tub is small and deep and has a bench seat. It's a perfect choice for an Asian-inspired design.

BELOW If you're looking for more than a warm soak, this freestanding model has 60 air jets that offer a "hot springs effect." Using a remote control, you can choose one of three massage settings. Both the pedestal and tub are available in different cast-acrylic colors, so you can mix or match them.

OPPOSITE TOP, LEFT AND RIGHT If space in your bathroom is limited, a corner tub may be the answer. This one has been molded with an integral skirt and measures 60 x 36 x 20 in.

OPPOSITE BOTTOM, LEFT AND RIGHT Another corner unit, this one has separate tub filler and handshower docking stations. Spa options are available on compact units, so don't let space limit your design.

just try it

When you're shopping, look online, but also visit showrooms where you can sit in a tub to gauge its size and your level of comfort.

ABOVE LEFT Ergonomics are important in today's tub designs. This soaker comes with a neck pillow.

ABOVE Lightweight acrylic can replace heavy cast iron in a reproduction of a popular vintage style.

LEFT Similar to a sink, a drop-in tub may be lowered into a deck or mounted underneath it. Paneling or tiling is required to finish the exterior.

OPPOSITE This modern design is a sleeker version of a classic style.

replace or refinish?

Old bathtubs may show signs of wear and tear eventually, or the color fades or becomes outdated. Then comes the decision—refinish or replace?

- **Replacing.** A new tub is not necessarily expensive, but factor in the cost of installing it (after removing the old one) and the cost goes up. After you have shut off the water supply to the tub and fished out the drain and overflow assembly, you've got to separate the tub from the wall and the floor, which may require some demolition. If you're removing a standard 30- x 60-in. tub, you may be able to carry it out sideways through doors and hallways, or even through a window. Another solution may be to break up the tub using a saw or sledgehammer, a messy, time-consuming task.

- **Refinishing.** Some of the hassle involved in replacing a tub can make refinishing a better idea if your old one is in fairly good condition. Professionals can repair minor chips and cracks in enameled or porcelainized tubs and reglaze the surface. The refurbishing will last about 5 years. Another, somewhat longer-lasting solution is a tub liner. This involves applying a form-fitting acrylic sheet, or liner, over the old tub. The liner is fabricated from one of literally hundreds of molds made of standard old tubs. The installer takes detailed measurements of your tub to make a seamless match. Upon installation, a special adhesive binds the liner to the tub without disturbing the adjacent walls and existing plumbing.

spa-style tubs take pampering to dazzling heights

OPPOSITE TOP A graceful oval tub with a beveled rim suits the bath's traditional styling. A generous granite deck provides ample open storage space.

OPPOSITE BOTTOM You can use bubble bath, bath salts, and oils with an air-jetted tub, but they are not recommended for use with water-jetted models.

RIGHT For ultimate pampering, choose an extra-deep design.

BELOW Simplicity is key to creating a relaxing environment. Here the view is the only distraction.

Go Green

Reduce indoor air pollution and ventilate the room naturally with energy-efficient windows.

Some people prefer the efficient, invigorating experience of a shower to a slow soak in a tub. And there are plenty of features to make showering just as special and luxurious. In fact, the feature-filled shower is so popular that in some households it has replaced the tub altogether.

The most common, most economical—and least convenient—shower is the one that's combined with the bathtub. If you've stepped in and out of the tub, done battle with the shower curtain, or tried to keep a shower door clean, you'll be aware that a separate shower enclosure is a luxury in itself, filled with extra features or not.

showers

You'll need space—and a hefty budget—for a large luxury shower, but some compact models are quite reasonable. Fiberglass or acrylic prefabricated units are generally 73 inches high and 36 inches deep; typical widths are 32, 36, or 48 inches. Don't let the word "prefabricated" fool you. True, some of these units are very basic, equipped with no more than a standard showerhead and a little soap dish. But other prefabricated models offer luxury features such as multiple showerheads, body sprays, jets, steam capabilities, chromotherapy options, TVs, and DVD and CD players.

Custom-designed showers often boast similar luxury features, but their enclosures are usually more luxurious, with walls covered in stone, ceramic tiles, or in some contemporary bathrooms, even glass, metal, or concrete.

fit to be tiled

Before tiling a storage niche in a tub or shower wall, measure your liquid-soap and hair-product bottles to make sure they'll fit.

OPPOSITE LEFT This seamless custom design is extravagant in its simplicity. A roof window showers the space with sunlight.

OPPOSITE RIGHT A showerhead and a hand-held sprayer supply variety and convenience.

ABOVE A glass shower enclosure keeps this handsome tile and stone unit on view, even from the master bedroom.

RIGHT A prefabricated shower can be fully loaded with spa features. This unit fits neatly into a corner—perfect for a small area.

more water?

Today's shower amenities are very appealing, but to function properly, spa features such as body sprays and jets require an adequate water supply, without which your luxurious "water experience" might be abruptly curtailed. Talk to your plumber about a larger or additional water heater or a booster pump, or check out low-flow body sprays that use less water to pamper you.

relaxation's a spray away

OPPOSITE LEFT A half wall supplies a semi-partition between the walk-in shower and the toilet area in this room.

OPPOSITE TOP Slate tile and wood evoke a sense of nature here. Both the tub and shower are jetted for maximum pampering.

OPPOSITE BOTTOM RIGHT Removing a closet yielded space for a shower in a bedroom that has been converted into a bath.

RIGHT This walk-in shower is well lit with fixtures that arc specified for installation in a wet area.

keep it sparklin'

Use a squeegee on glass partitions and doors after each shower to avoid messy-looking streaks.

LEFT Wall-mounted fittings with a brushed-chrome, modern industrial look have the clean lines called for by this Zen-inspired design.

ABOVE Refined yet simple floor-mounted fittings accessorize this freestanding bathing vessel, sculpted from natural stone, perfectly.

BELOW The antique-bronze finish on this arc-top faucet set blends handsomely into a bath with earth-tone tiles and Old World charm.

LEFT Deck-mounted fittings, including a separate sprayer, in a satin-nickel finish add a dash of glamour to the tub's solid-surface surround. Lever handles are a good choice for children and seniors.

BELOW This "French telephone" style tub set has polished-chrome cross handles and a body sprayer, all trimmed with enamel.

the beautification of the bathroom extends to every element, right down to the fittings. As a result, today's faucets are good-looking, durable, and hassle free. New washerless models won't drip, and brass valves won't wear out. But beware of lightweight faucets with plastic parts. They do wear out—quickly. For the tub, you'll need to choose between wall-mount or deck-mount fittings. Choices abound for finishes and styles, too. Chrome is the

fittings

most familiar, but brass, nickel, bronze, pewter, and enamels are also popular. Brushed or satin-matte finishes are easier to maintain because, unlike glossy polished finishes, they don't show scratches and water spots as easily. Styles range from Victorian to traditional to sleek and modern. For design continuity, make sure all fittings harmonize with one another and with the overall design of the room.

ABOVE LEFT A hand-held sprayer makes it easy to rinse off from head to toe. The wall-mounted slide and grab bar lets you adjust the height of the shower to your comfort level. You can leave it in the stationary position, too.

LEFT Shower tiles can be used alone or in a configuration of any number of them. Install them in shower walls or ceilings.

OPPOSITE TOP RIGHT This wall-mounted design pivots so you can aim water where you need it.

OPPOSITE BOTTOM RIGHT A rain showerhead offers a gentle yet invigorating spray of water.

BELOW This combination light-and-water fixture has a semitransparent cover that brings a touch of high fashion into the shower. It conceals a stainless-steel showerhead.

showerhead settings

There's no such thing as a boring shower these days—at least there doesn't need to be. Even reasonably priced single showerheads come with two or more special features—massaging, pulsating sprays that pound muscles to relieve soreness, refreshing cascades of water, or gentle flows that feel like a summer rain. Hand-held sprays, also reasonably priced, direct a stream of water exactly where you want it to go, and they usually offer a choice of spray settings. Sophisticated style comes at all price levels, too.

Multiple showerheads kick things up several notches. Positioned at different heights on the wall, they direct the water where you need it, providing a stand-up whirlpool massage. In some showers, jets can be placed on more than one wall to create a whole "body spa." If you can't afford in-the-wall jets, there are kits that convert a shower into a hydromassage center without replumbing.

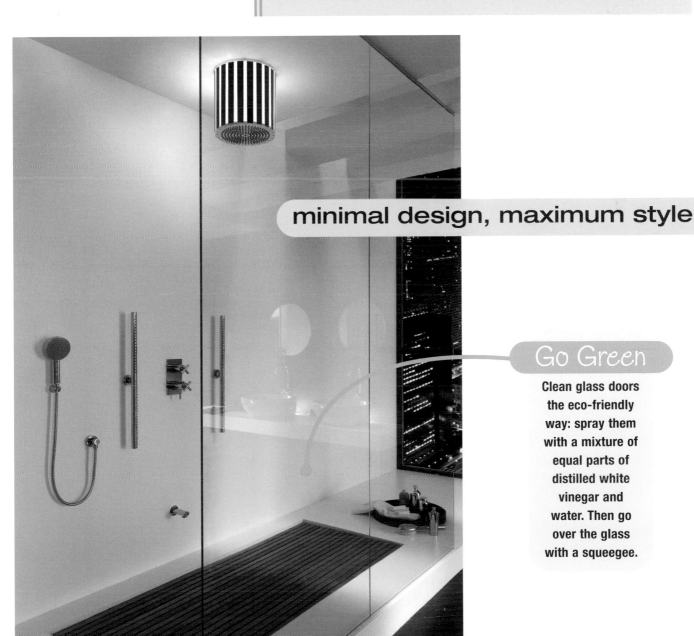

minimal design, maximum style

Go Green

Clean glass doors the eco-friendly way: spray them with a mixture of equal parts of distilled white vinegar and water. Then go over the glass with a squeegee.

heat your spa's floor

Treat yourself to even more pampering—underfoot. Traditional radiant-heating systems consist of hot-water-carrying pipes embedded in a concrete slab. The water warms the concrete, which radiates heat into the room. It is expensive, but efficient. A new version of radiant heating, electric systems do away with the piping and slab, allowing you to bring radiant heat to a smaller area, such as your bathroom. Available from a number of manufacturers, the systems consist of a mesh that contains a heating element, pictured right. All you have to do is staple the mesh to the subfloor, and then apply ceramic tile in thinset. Most systems are used as auxiliary heating.

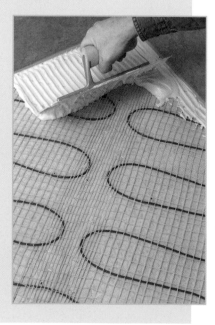

ABOVE A refreshing shower awaits after a sauna in this luxurious at-home spa.

OPPOSITE LEFT Heated towels are ready as you step out of the shower or tub. Radiant heating was installed under the floor tiles.

OPPOSITE RIGHT This rain canopy can shower you with light and color (inset). Color is a personal choice, so choose one that either relaxes or invigorates you.

spa amenities

There are many ways to make your bathroom truly luxurious. You might break the budget if you choose every one of them. Aim for affordable luxury by splurging on one or two favorite features, such as

- A TV that's visible from the tub—relax and watch a movie while you soak.
- A CD player in the shower—pick the tunes that rev your spirits in the morning or relax you at night.
- Shower jets that target specific muscles—get a massage whenever you ache.
- A built-in tanning feature—keep skin moist by tanning while you shower.
- Access to the outdoors. Equip an adjacent deck or patio with a hot tub you can use year-round.

The latest spa amenity? Chromatherapy.

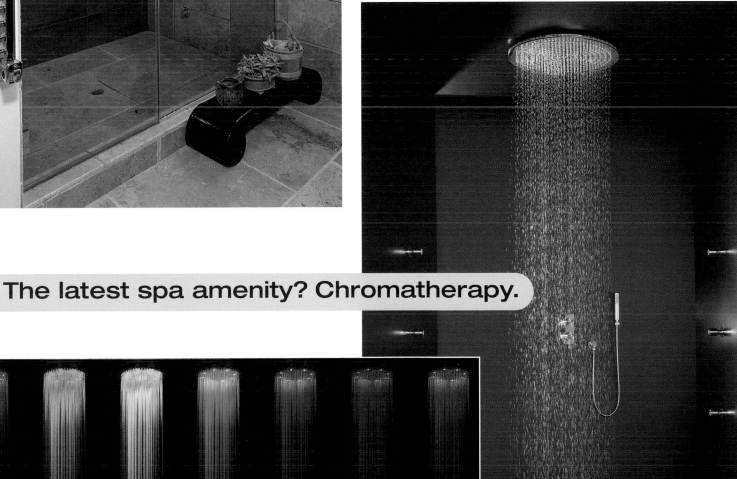

The Surfaces

I deally, the floors, walls, and countertops in your bathroom perform two important services at the same time—they establish the stylish look of your choice, and they provide easy-clean surfaces that stand up to wear and tear and resist moisture and humidity. There are many materials from which to chose—stone, ceramic tile, glass, concrete, solid-surfacing, plastic laminate, wood, and metal—and most of them come in a mind-boggling array of sizes, shapes, and colors. The following information and portfolio of photographs will help you make a selection that's right for you.

- **stone**
- **ceramic tile**
- **glass**
- **concrete**
- **synthetics**
- **wood**
- **metal**

Cool stone makes this bathroom a modern classic. Smooth glass surfaces—the clear shower surround and the frosted doors on the front of the custom vanity—add to the design's contemporary appeal.

nothing beats stone for luxurious beauty and durability in the bath. Granite and marble are perennial favorites, and limestone and slate are fast catching up. In small doses, say on a countertop, stone blends with any decorating style. Large expanses generally produce a cool, contemporary look; but marble, favored by the Victorians, is often used in period or traditional designs.

The beauty of stone derives from its grain and infinite variety of vibrant colors. Finishes vary from glossy and polished, to honed and matte, to tumbled—an aged, weathered look that has lately gained favor. Polished stone is slippery when wet. A honed or tumbled finish is safer for bathroom floors. Soapstone, which ages to a rich charcoal gray that you may remember from the counter of your high-school chemistry lab, is gaining popularity, as are slate, available in a variety of surprisingly bright shades, and creamy-beige limestone. No two pieces of stone look alike, which is part of its appeal; if you're seeking uniformity, consider engineered stone, an up-and-coming material created by binding stone chips and powders with resins. Nonporous and easy-care, engineered stone comes in a wide range of colors, including blues and yellows not found in natural materials.

The quality, durability, and even porosity of stones can vary greatly depending on where they are quarried and who is selling them. Seek out a reputable dealer and shop carefully.

RIGHT Blue-gray marble accommodates a pair of black above-counter lavs. The gray slate-tile floor handsomely ties the look together.

stone

BELOW FAR LEFT A stone basin sits atop a counter with a chiseled edge. The design has a strong rustic yet refined appeal.

BELOW MIDDLE As this tub deck demonstrates, stone can come in colors other than earth tones. If you can't find the real thing, opt for a synthetic look-alike.

BELOW RIGHT Honed pebbles, as seen on this shower floor, look natural and feel good underfoot.

ABOVE Large-scale marble tiles, installed tightly with an almost seamless look, keep this design simple yet rich.

LEFT Stone patterns vary—some are subtle while others, like this countertop, are pronounced. The oil-rubbed faucet picks up the stone's deepest tone.

LEFT White marble with gray or black veining has classic good looks and is readily available in a slab or as tiles.

OPPOSITE TOP The blue vanity, sleek brushed-chrome hardware, and expansive stone surfaces bring a contemporary sensibility to this room.

OPPOSITE BOTTOM Brown marble complements the chocolate color of the wood-paneled tub surround.

stone surfacing will increase the value of your bath

how to care for natural stone

Some people like the look of a little wear and tear with their stone surfacing, but others, having spent a bundle on the stone, want it to look next to perfect. As a surface for the bath, natural stone is almost perfect—but not quite. Most stone is hard, durable, and water-resistant. But even extra-hard granite may stain if exposed to harsh chemicals or acidic substances, and it requires a periodic application of a sealant.

Marble and limestone are beautiful in the bath, but they stain and scratch easily. Be cautious with hair colorings and other chemicals, and wipe up spills right away. Use wax to protect a marble finish, and safeguard limestone with a sealant.

Protect all types of stone from gritty dirt, which dulls finishes over time, by sweeping regularly and damp-mopping with a small amount of mild, nonacidic soap or cleaner. Too much soap will leave a film. Polished stone may benefit from a periodic application of a commercial polish to enhance luster and beef up protection, and repair kits are available for some stains and scratches.

veins glorious

Stick with stone with subtle veining for a low-key look. A busy pattern will detract from other decorative elements.

LEFT Standard 4 x 4-in. ceramic tiles in several shades of green form an interesting random tone-on-tone pattern here.

RIGHT For a clean look, you can install an under-mounted sink beneath a tiled countertop. These ceramic tiles have a slightly rough surface that resembles stone.

BELOW Mix sizes, shapes, and finishes for visual interest. The floor tiles are matte, providing better traction.

ceramic

ceramic tile has been used to beautify bathrooms for many centuries, and it remains a good choice today. It is durable—more so than some types of natural stone, in fact—and impervious to stains and moisture. Ceramic tile is manufactured in many sizes and shapes—from tiny hexagonal mosaics to 12-inch squares—and in a wealth of colors—neutrals and earth tones, pastels, brights, and iridescents. This dazzling variety permits personal expression with one-of-a-kind designs and configurations. Ceramic trim pieces and decorative borders can also create interesting effects and even mimic architectural detailing.

Glazed, shiny tiles work well on counters and walls but are not suitable for floors in the bath. For safety, choose a floor tile with a gritty, nonslip surface.

Ceramic tiles themselves are a snap to clean, but grout lines pose a challenge. You can keep grout sparkling

tile

by treating it with a sealer and then cleaning it regularly with a mild bleach solution. Even easier, use colored grout.

When you shop, tell your dealer where you will use the tile, how much traffic it will get, and how long you need it to last. An experienced dealer will help you make the right choice.

ABOVE These glossy tiles add a textural look to the walls that suits the overall design of this powder room.

LEFT Small mosaic tiles are an easy way to add pattern. The off-white, tan, brown, and taupe tiles here pair well with the brushed-nickel finish on the faucet and the tiled surface surrounding the bath, which is reflected in the mirror.

ABOVE, ABOVE RIGHT, AND RIGHT Mosaic tile gives you the opportunity to be creative. Design a mural, such as this colorful display, above; evoke a retro look, as seen in the floor tile, above right; or devise a decorative pattern for the floor, such as a tile "rug," right.

sheets, in fact

You'll be happy to know that these tiny tiles may come in sheets, making them easier to install on a large surface.

RIGHT Tiny tiles can be made of ceramic, stone, glass, or metal. These have a luminous quality, reflecting the light in the room.

BELOW RIGHT Walls finished with tiny tiles in various shades of blue look refreshing surrounding this tub.

glazed or unglazed

Ceramic tile is composed of clay, water, and other naturally occurring substances fired at high heat.

- **Glazed tiles** are covered with a ceramic coating that gives the tile body its color and finish. The glaze effectively repels moisture, stains, bacteria, allergens, and odors, but it also creates a shiny, potentially slippery surface. The higher the glaze, the less appropriate for use on floors. Glazed tiles are easy to clean, which is an important consideration in a room that requires daily maintenance.

- **Unglazed tiles** look natural, rough, and rustic because they derive their texture and color from clay rather than from a colored coating. Unglazed quarry tiles in rich beiges, browns, and rust are typical of the look. They are most often used on floors where their thickness and density make them especially durable and slip-proof. Some unglazed tiles are stain resistant, but most require periodic sealing.

shapes and patterns

Play it safe with basic tile shapes and patterns as seen below, or create a one-of-a-kind design with a unique layout combined with accent and border tiles.

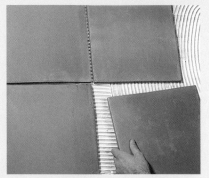

The basic floor tile measures 12 x 12 in. with a ⅛- to ¼-in. grout joint.

Sheet-mounted tile will look like individual mosaic tiles when installed.

Rectangular tiles can be used to create basket-weave patterns.

Combining different shapes allows you to create unique patterns.

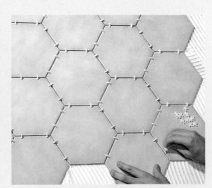

Hexagon-shaped tiles create an interlocked pattern.

Multicolor and multisize tiles are available in sheets.

most installations are fairly easy d-i-y projects

LEFT Cobalt-blue floor tiles look dramatic in a stark white room. The color plays off the mosaic tiles that frame the vanity mirror.

BELOW LEFT A border of standard 2 x 2-in. tiles in green, blue, and white inexpensively adds a lot of visual punch to the vanity and the shower here.

BELOW The smaller the tile, the more slip-resistant the floor. That's because more grout lines provide better traction underfoot—a paramount concern in a wet room.

new looks

This classic "brick" style has moved beyond traditional glossy white to more colors, sizes, and finishes.

Go Green

A recycled-glass countertop is an eco-friendly alternative to nonrenewable resources, such as stone.

glass

glass is an exciting surface for sinks, countertops, walls, and even floors. Clear or colored glass sinks and counters are showing up more often, as are glass tiles. Available in many sizes and in translucent, transparent, or opaque finishes, glass tiles offer an amazing range of color—shimmering jewel-tones, frosted pastels, ambers with the look of carnival glass, and dark shades shot through with silver or gold. Large, smooth glass tiles may be too slippery for a bathroom floor, but smaller pieces with many grout lines can provide a safer, gritty surface.

Glass is durable and easy to clean, but installation is costly. If you find that a large expanse of glass tiles exceeds your budget, consider combining them with less pricey synthetics, ceramic tiles, or even wood. Use the glass as a border or cover only a small area, such as a vanity top.

Glass block, an architectural staple in the 1930s and '40s, has made a comeback in bathrooms. Because they transmit 80 percent of available natural light, these translucent blocks are ideal substitutes for windows when privacy is desired, and can also be used as shower walls or privacy partitions without compromising light or openness. Available in many square or rectangular sizes, glass block also offers several finishes and textures.

ABOVE Jewel-tone, iridescent glass tiles look exotic and shimmer under the light in this bathroom.

LEFT AND ABOVE The mirrored vanity, left, embellishes the glitter and glamour, while a smooth glass countertop paired with a metal lav, above, looks sleek and contemporary.

RIGHT A wall of glass block serves as a light-filtering partition between a bath and a shower area.

ABOVE Mixing glass tiles with stone surfaces makes an elegant, minimalist statement here. The wall-mounted lav and faucets draw the eye to the tile.

ABOVE RIGHT The brushed-brass hardware and turquoise cups pick up similar tones in the iridescent glass tiles.

RIGHT Small glass tiles in various tones of blue form a border in this otherwise all-white shower.

OPPOSITE Glass—including the shower enclosure, a tall mirror, and the lav and console—combines with light-color surfaces to open up a small space.

cool glass is a hot surfacing material in today's bath

LEFT Concrete is easy to mold and shape. Here it was used to fabricate a long, trough-style lav in a contemporary bathroom.

OPPOSITE A long concrete-topped vanity has plenty of space for grooming. The floor features concrete-cast tiles.

LEFT This large soaking tub has an organic look, reinforced by natural materials throughout the space.

ABOVE A solid-concrete console supports two vessel-style lavs in a master bath.

Considered daring and unconventional only a dozen years ago, concrete is now gaining wide acceptance for surfaces in the bath, as well as for tubs and showers. Surprisingly, this mundane material can be formed into graceful shapes and topped with several types of finishes—rough and rustic, glossy and polished, or subtly glowing. If you were expecting a boring, sidewalk-like surface, you'll find the color selection surprising, too. Although many homeowners prefer muted, earthy shades, such as ivory, pearl gray, or sand, vivid hues are also available, depending on the skill and inventiveness of the concrete fabricator.

Treated with chemicals, pigments, and epoxy coatings—or mixed with bits of metal or colored glass—concrete also takes on the look of stone. This potential for uniqueness is part of this material's appeal.

Concrete is a natural choice, of course, for a minimalist or contemporary decorating scheme, but used in conjunction with more conventional elements, such as wood or ceramic tile, it is equally at home in a traditional-style bathroom. Concrete counters are not available off the shelf, nor is this a job for a do-it-yourselfer. To assure good results, you will need a specialist to fabricate the concrete for you. Although concrete itself is not expensive, the professional fabrication will set you back, in total, about as much as natural stone surfacing would. Still, it is important that you seek out an experienced contractor or fabricator. And before you make a decision to go with concrete, ask the fabricator to show you a counter, sink, or tub surround that has been in place for some time.

concrete

unseamly

A pair of curved-bottom integral concrete sinks keeps this area free of grime-collecting seams.

concrete designs can be earthy and sophisticated

ABOVE LEFT This countertop is an aggregate mix of particles and concrete. Grinding and polishing brings the aggregate to the surface.

ABOVE AND RIGHT This unique bathroom makes creative use of concrete. The shower floor and tub deck, above, are also fabricated in concrete. The vanity, right, features concrete sinks that angle outward to mimic the shape of the cabinet.

LEFT A stand-alone concrete soaking tub, which has been molded in one piece, makes a statement.

concrete facts

If you're afraid that a concrete counter or tub surround in your bathroom will resemble the floor in your garage or the sidewalk outside your house, take another look. The colors, finishes, and special effects possible with concrete are quite varied, and none of them resemble a nasty garage floor. In fact, even a simple concrete application without any bells and whistles appears sleek and streamlined.

If it is treated with a sealant, concrete will stand up well to wear and moisture, provided you wipe up spills right away, clean the surface regularly with a nonabrasive cleanser, and renew the sealant twice a year. Hairline cracks do tend to develop, but they are generally not structural and can be easily repaired. And not to worry—most experts say concrete gets more beautiful as it ages.

ABOVE A concrete-topped vanity has been acid-stained a brilliant turquoise. The matching flooring is scored concrete.

dry idea

Because it is impermeable, you can extend solid-surfacing material to the wall around a tub or shower.

ABOVE This roomy tub has been set into a surround fabricated from solid-surfacing material—a synthetic with solid-through color.

BELOW A tough but affordable synthetic countertop makes sense in a bathroom designed for kids.

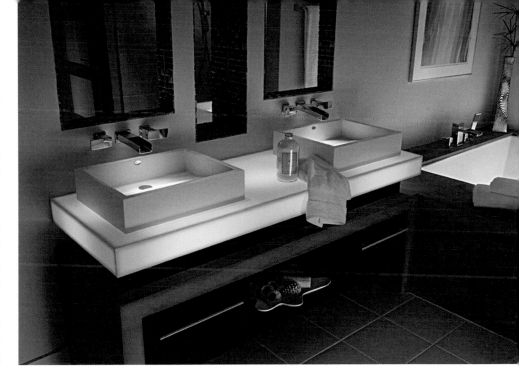

ince the 1930s, when plastic laminate first hit the market-place, manufacturers have been hard at work creating surfacing products that resemble stone but cost less money and need less maintenance. Available in hundreds of colors, patterns, and finishes, laminates are the least costly of these synthetics, and post-formed, ready-to-install laminate countertops are even more economical. Laminate flooring mimics wood, tile, or stone and provides easy-clean durability underfoot, as does resilient vinyl flooring, another cost-conscious choice, which is available in a multitude of patterns. Introduced about 30 years ago, solid

synthetics

surfacing—a tough, color-through material made of polyesters or acrylics—can look like stone but is more malleable and can be formed into many shapes, including architectural edges and integral sinks. Composites mix quartz compounds with man-made resins to create surfaces that are nearly impervious to wear and tear. In a recent technological advance, some synthetic countertops offer an antibacterial layer that repels mold and mildew.

OPPOSITE Resilient sheet-vinyl flooring is often inexpensive and easy to install.

TOP RIGHT A special type of solid-surfacing material offers enough transparency to allow light to pass through it for a dynamic effect.

RIGHT This laminate flooring offers the look of natural stone, but it's warmer and softer underfoot.

fabulous fakes

When it comes to bathroom surfacing materials, the real thing isn't always the best thing. True, nothing beats the beauty and luxury of stone. But if your budget precludes it, why not check out solid-surfacing or composite materials? Both look almost as good as stone, most applications cost slightly less, and the materials have been engineered to resist the chemicals and acidic substances that can stain marble or granite. Because the color goes all the way through solid-surfacing material, scratches and nicks can be gently sanded away without leaving a scar— a big advantage over both high-end stone and low-cost laminate, which once scratched, are difficult to repair.

Solid-surfacing material does not require any special treatment, just regular swipes with a damp cloth.

Composites, which are made of quartz particles combined with acrylic resins, duplicate the pigmentation, swirls, and veins of natural materials, particularly granite. The color range incorporates both earth tones and brights, such as blue, green, red, and yellow. Also a low-maintenance product, a composite surface is extremely hard and durable, resists scratches and stains, and unlike stone, does not need to be sealed either for protection or to enhance its shine.

LEFT This homeowner chose a quiet color for the countertop to let the room's dramatic Mexican tiles take the spotlight.

OPPOSITE LEFT AND RIGHT Synthetics, such as solid-surfacing material and composites, can be cut out to accommodate an undermounted lav. The terrazzo lookalike, left, is solid-surfacing material, while the other countertop, right, is a quartz composite.

RIGHT Because a quartz-composite material contains almost all stone, it's hard to tell the difference between it and the real thing.

shiny or matte

Quartz-composite material comes in polished and honed finishes, but the latter will need a bit more daily care.

stone look-alikes offer the luxury of easy care

LEFT The variety of colors and patterns that are available have increased the popularity of man-made materials.

BELOW A laminate floor that mimics the look of light slate will cost less and require a minimum amount of maintenance.

RIGHT Plastic laminate is a classic material, and it offers the greatest range of colors.

man-made materials offer style without the upkeep

Go Green

If you're considering a laminate floor, look for one that has low urea-formaldehyde emissions.

laminate—a perennial favorite

Plastic laminate's low cost and huge range of colors, patterns, and finishes make it a perennially popular and practical surfacing material. Laminate counters are susceptible to stains and scratches and do not last forever, but the availability of the material and the ease and economy of replacing it counteract these minor drawbacks. To minimize marks, choose a matte finish and light color, which mask signs of wear.

many bath surfacing materials have a rich look, but none of them can compete with the gleaming and familiar warmth of wood. Conventional wisdom has long dictated that wood and the moisture in the bath should not mix, but there are ways to make it work.

Underfoot, wood is friendlier and more resilient—and warmer—than cool, hard natural stone or ceramic tile. Any wood species successfully used for flooring is appropriate for the bath provided it is installed and prepared properly. However, do keep in mind that certain woods resist moisture, and the decay that results from it, better than others, notably cedar, redwood, and teak. Narrow floor boards—2 inches wide, for example—work better in the bathroom than wide boards. The skinny strips absorb less moisture and swell and shrink slightly less than wider boards. To protect any wood floor from the effects of moisture and humidity, apply several coats of polyurethane, or try one of the new sealants called watershed protectors, all of which repel water better than an oiled or waxed finish. However, even a protected floor can be damaged by standing water, so wipe up spills right away and use a bath mat when you step out of the bathtub or shower.

wood

Finish wood countertops with the same sealants you would use on the floor, or invest in a ready-made, pretreated butcher-block counter. There is some evidence that natural substances in wood prevent the buildup of bacteria, a bonus for a bathroom countertop. Resist the impulse to cover the shower in wood— the constant exposure to water takes a serious toll, even on moisture-resistant species that have been sealed.

Vacuum or sweep wood floors and wash regularly with a barely damp mop and mild cleanser or special wood soap. Stay ahead of moisture damage by renewing protective finishes every few years and installing a ventilation system to whisk away humidity.

OPPOSITE A practical choice in a bathroom, engineered wood—which has a plywood base—holds up against moisture.

LEFT AND BELOW LEFT Teak is a tropical hardwood with natural oils that make it durable even when it's exposed to moisture. Combined here with stone, it gives the sense of an outdoor room.

BELOW Wood paneling in a bathroom looks cozy, but you'll have to protect it from warping by applying varnish or a clear sealant, which will need periodic maintenance. It may be more sensible to limit wood paneling to a powder room.

metal

further proof that bathroom design has come a long way from the bland box with three white fixtures is the appearance of metal as a surfacing material. Frequently used in smart-looking kitchens on appliances, and occasionally on countertops, metal seems an unlikely candidate for bathroom use. But it is coming on strong lately, especially in the form of tiles and on walls, as well. Although this cutting-edge material is practically indestructible, which is an advantage, it is also cold to the touch and to the eye, which is not especially desirable. To keep this coolness from dominating, designers typically use metal sparingly, often in combination with softer, warmer materials. For example, an expanse of metal tiles might be offset by a limestone or wood floor, or intermixed with ceramic tile. For a really innovative look, try a vanity counter in copper, bronze, or brass.

Metal is an especially sanitary surface—it repels bacteria and discourages the growth of mildew. It doesn't absorb stains, won't crack, and it cleans easily. In time, all types of metal will scratch, particularly copper. To mask marks, choose a brushed, textured, or matte finish. Copper can be sealed against discoloration, or you can let it age gracefully to a burnished patina.

LEFT A wall of metal tiles adds Hollywood-style glamour to this powder room, especially when it reflects light.

BELOW A copper tub has a luxurious appeal. It will take on a patina over time. To retain its original color, dry it after each use.

OPPOSITE This design combines a cool stainless-steel vanity with a warm amber-color glass counter and lav for visual and tactile interest.

metal is a new decorative option for the room

bathroom lavs have changed more dramatically in recent years than any other design element, taking on new and intriguing shapes, vivid colors, and unconventional materials. White, bone, and black are still big sellers, but if you want to get adventurous, there are plenty of alternatives.

When you shop, focus on your budget and the type, size, and style of your bath, lest you be seduced by a fabulous, expensive lav that won't

lavs

suit your needs. For a family or master bath, where two or more people greet the day at the same time, you'll need two lavs, a roomy counter, and storage below; if space is tight, a freestanding or wall-hung model will free up floor area. Unless your bath is contemporary or eclectic in style, you may want to save exotic styles and materials for a guest bath or a powder room.

Most sinks are still made of porcelain, glazed vitreous china, or enameled cast iron—durable materials that are resistant to water, stains, and mildew. Innovative shapes and colors are possible with solid surfacing, cultured stone, concrete, metal, and glass. But stone and concrete should be sealed or they will stain, and glass and metal are susceptible to scratches.

You can expect to pay about $100 for a basic white or beige drop-in or pedestal model; for colored or integral lavs, add a couple of hundred to that. Ornate pedestal sinks or designer lavs in unusual materials or vivid colors run from $300 to about $700. For custom-made, hand-painted, and one-of-a-kind lavs, you'll have to part with many times that amount.

OPPOSITE TOP LEFT This vessel lav's hand-painted pattern is based on a sixteenth-century Chinese porcelain dish.

OPPOSITE TOP RIGHT Graceful in form, a classic pedestal sink is always in style

OPPOSITE BOTTOM His and her porcelain china sinks display a decorative beveled edge.

TOP LEFT An exposed-apron lav has an extra-deep bowl. Its nostalgic look pairs handsomely with this Mexican-tile bath.

TOP RIGHT This vitreous-china, above-counter model is double-glazed and fired for durability.

BELOW To create this design, skeletons of fish etched out of pieces of copper and brass have been fused between layers of glass to achieve the look of burnished fossils.

LEFT A new design, this lav's vintage-inspired wrought-iron pedestal is evocative of the ornate furniture of the late Victorian era.

RIGHT Traditional styling with details that resemble crown molding distinguish this pedestal sink.

BELOW LEFT A simple white sink and cone-shaped cabinet make an ultramodern statement.

BELOW MIDDLE Made of hammered copper, this above-counter bowl rests on a slab of rough-hewn French limestone.

BELOW RIGHT Two console-style sinks resemble furniture in this high-end master bath.

OPPOSITE TOP AND BOTTOM A lav can be mounted on a small table or set into a console for a furniture-like appearance.

the many looks of today's pedestal and console lavs

ABOVE A self-rimming lav is set into a countertop.

ABOVE RIGHT A vessel-style lav sits on top of the counter.

LEFT An integral sink is fabricated seamlessly from the same material as the countertop.

OPPOSITE TOP This lav has been dropped into the glass countertop, which has been raised about 7 in. above the top of the cabinet.

pros and cons of mounting styles

Before you chose a lav, decide which type of installation best satisfies your needs, budget, and design preferences.

- **Drop-in** lavs (also called self-rimming or rimmed) are readily available, easy to install, and provided you choose white or beige, inexpensive. Disadvantages? The rim doesn't protect countertops from splashes if the basin is shallow. Also, grime can accumulate under the outside edge.

- **Freestanding** or wall-mounted models take up little space, making them ideal for small or accessible baths—wheelchairs slide right under some of them. The down-side—plumbing is exposed; there's little or no counter area; and under-counter storage is nonexistent.

- **Under-mount** lavs, which are attached to the underside of a finished counter opening, maximize deck area, look sleek, and clean easily. However, the countertop material must be impervious to water. Standard laminate is unsuitable, and wood, unless properly sealed, will soon rot, peel, or buckle.

- **Integral** lavs, also sleek looking and easy to clean, are low cost if made from cultured stone or concrete; solid surfacing and natural stone are pricier. The downside—most integral bowls are shallow and prone to splashing unless they are paired with low-profile faucets.

- **Above-counter,** or vessel, lavs are stylish and trendy and require wall- or deck-mounted faucets. They can be costly and delicate depending on the material you choose; installation may be expensive, too.

today's trends

- **Exotic materials.** Today, a lav can be made from just about any material that will hold water—stone, concrete, hand-blown or hand-painted glass, and many kinds of metal from stainless steel and copper to luxurious pewter, silver, and even gold. The newest trend is wood, a seemingly unlikely material. But according to manufacturers, wood lavs can be pretreated and sealed to resist warping, rotting, or buckling.

- **Lav furniture.** Chests of drawers, marble-topped wash stands, streamlined tables, fancy metal bases—all are turning up to hold lavs and act as vanities. Transform your own furniture into a one-of-a-kind piece or check manufacturers' offerings.

- **Color.** No longer content with white or beige, homeowners are asking for—and getting—color. Coexisting with the exotic-materials trend, the color revolution has introduced vivid reds and blues, deep greens, rich earth tones, and tropical shades such as mango, tangerine, and lime to the lav palette. In addition to solid colors, painted designs are available, usually as special orders.

- **Shapes.** Typical round and oval designs are available in all of the hot new colors and materials, of course. But you can also purchase or custom order rectangles, squares, long troughs, bowls, and any number of free-flowing sculpturesque configurations.

Go Green

Creating a totally eco-friendly bathroom? Consider a bamboo sink, which can sit on a countertop, vessel style, or you can mount it on the wall.

OPPOSITE TOP LEFT This rectangular countertop lav pairs well with minimalist or Modern decor.

OPPOSITE TOP RIGHT Elliptical and round shapes usually range in size from 14 to 17 in.

OPPOSITE BOTTOM A custom design, such as this stone sink, can be fabricated to your exact size.

TOP RIGHT This sink has been constructed of tough bamboo that has been grown without pesticides or fertilizer.

MIDDLE RIGHT A pinwheel of crescent shapes protrudes from the surface of this 15-in. glass lav in hue-shifting color.

BOTTOM RIGHT Colorful circles have been fused directly into the thickness of this low-iron clear-glass 18-in. bowl.

ABOVE This glass waterfall faucet has a 7.5-in tempered-glass dish that comes clear or in a color.

ABOVE RIGHT The blue and white floral motif of this ceramic faucet was inspired by a Ming vase.

RIGHT Metal and stone make a strong pair, hence the choice of this polished-chrome mixer.

FAR RIGHT A bronze faucet coordinates well with many of today's natural-stone surfaces.

OPPOSITE TOP For a traditional look, this centerset faucet features classic graceful curves and a satin-nickel finish.

it's fitting

A tall, single-lever faucet is the best style for a vessel lav. One with an angled spout causes less splashing.

lav faucets

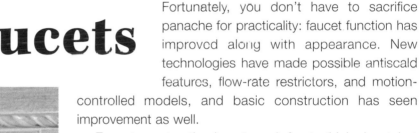

lthough basic, no-nonsense lav faucets are still widely available, most homeowners prefer to make a splash with more adventurous fittings and finishes. If you shop smart, you can bring home a beautiful faucet without breaking the bank.

Fortunately, you don't have to sacrifice panache for practicality: faucet function has improved along with appearance. New technologies have made possible antiscald features, flow-rate restrictors, and motion-controlled models, and basic construction has seen improvement as well.

Faucet construction is not much fun to think about, but the outer glamour of shapes and finishes will cease to please you if the innards fail. Compression valves, an older type of construction, use washers to control water flow; this is the least expensive type of construction but also the least reliable because washers frequently wear out and need replacing. Newer, washerless types include cartridge units, which are reliable but somewhat costly to repair, and ceramic-disc valves, which are very durable and nearly maintenance free. Solid-brass or brass-and-metal components are more reliable than plastic parts. Basic compression-valve fittings are downright cheap. If you ante up a little more for cartridge or ceramic-disc construction, you've made a smart investment. Having selected a faucet that won't need frequent repair or replacement, you can focus on sparkling finishes and alluring shapes, for which you could pay anywhere from a couple of hundred to thousands of dollars.

bronze age

An oil-rubbed bronze finish is expensive and can wear with heavy use. Play it safe—buy the best quality, which will retain its good looks.

faucet lingo

Want to be a savvy shopper? Buy a lav and faucet at the same time, coordinating them in style and making sure the fittings match the number of predrilled holes in the lav. Also, check that the faucet's spout reaches well into the basin.

- **Centerset fittings** require only one hole. They combine a spout and two handles that are set about 4 in. apart, center to center, in a single base.

- **Widespread fittings** require three predrilled holes. These faucets place hot- and cold-water controls 8 to 12 in. apart, center to center, with the spout generally in between them. Valves and spout appear to be separate.

- **Single-hole fittings** require one hole and condense the spout and control for both hot and cold water into one unit.

Any of these configurations can be **deck-** or **wall-mounted.** Deck-mounted fittings are installed into the area surrounding the basin—the rim—or the countertop. Wall-mounted fittings are installed into the wall behind the basin. In either case, the spout must be long enough to direct water into the center of the bowl.

OPPOSITE TOP LEFT Sleek crosshandles and a long spout coordinate with this wet-surface lavatory.

OPPOSITE TOP RIGHT A single-control faucet fits neatly behind this conical above-counter bowl.

LEFT Decorative finials top these faucet handles. This three-hole, widespread design wears a dramatic black-iron finish.

ABOVE This centerset faucet can be installed into a sink deck or countertop that has a single hole.

RIGHT A widespread faucet has been mounted onto the wall to accommo-date a vessel.

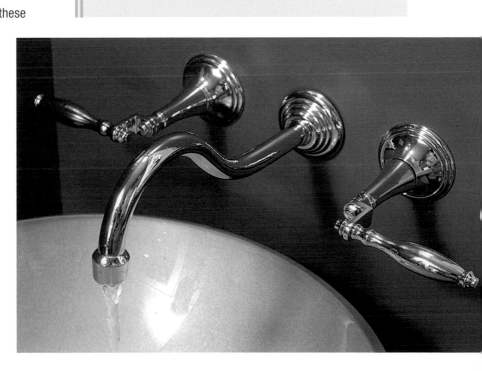

ABOVE LEFT Lever-style scroll handles and a high-arc spout wear a brushed-bronze finish.

ABOVE RIGHT A widespread faucet set in French gold looks elegant with this pedestal lav.

LEFT This antique-bronze design has Old World appeal.

finding the right one

As you shop for faucets you will find that fancy finishes flourish. Chrome, an old standby, is durable, affordable, and tarnish resistant, and it always looks good. But if you don't mind a little extra expense and upkeep, you can add big sparkle to your bath with brass, nickel, bronze, colored baked-on epoxy porcelain, stainless steel—even gold, silver, or platinum. On polished finishes, water spots and scratches stand out, requiring more care and polishing than brushed, satin, or matte treatments. Most finishes show wear over time, especially if you use abrasive cleansers. A relatively new development, a physical vapor deposition (PVD) finish, increases costs by about 30 percent but promises a lasting shine.

you have your pick from a variety of finishes

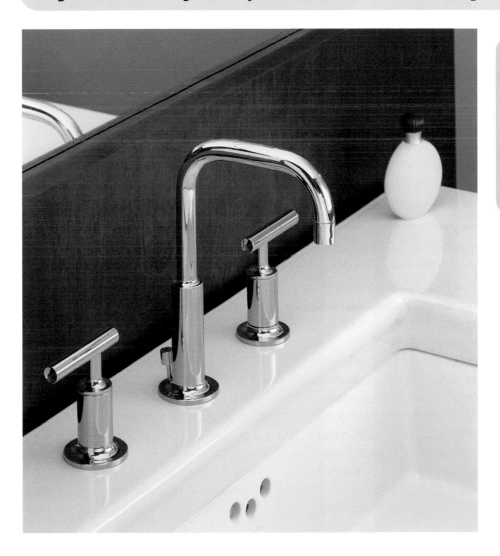

ABOVE LEFT This bamboo-inspired design in satin nickel has an unusual water spout.

ABOVE RIGHT Hammered nickel is an understated finish that coordinates with a sleek look.

LEFT This Modern geometric style gleams in polished nickel.

the style's in the toilet—and that's a good thing

LEFT This one-piece, low-profile toilet suits contemporary design.

ABOVE A two-piece device can be purchased with a standard-size or elongated bowl.

OPPOSITE TOP One innovative feature of this model is the specially engineered hinge system that closes the lid softly and quietly.

OPPOSITE BOTTOM Ordering a suite of fixtures, rather than individual pieces, allows you to match colors precisely. Variations can occur, even in neutral tones, such as white, beige, or gray.

gravity or pressure

Another choice faces you when you go shopping—will you use gravity or pressure to flush your new toilet?

- **Gravity-flush** toilets are the familiar kind—water from the tank flushes the bowl clean. But because today's gravity-flush toilets are restricted to 1.6 gallons of water or less per flush—as low as 1.28 gallons in newer, more water-efficient models—more than one flush has been necessary to clear the bowl. However, manufacturers have addressed this problem, and flushing efficiency has improved.

- **Pressure-assist** toilets rely on water pressure in the line to compress air, which then works with a small amount of water to blast the bowl clean. This more-efficient flush uses less water, but the toilets are more expensive, more difficult to repair, and noisier than gravity-fed models.

bidets

bidets are fixtures for personal hygiene that came to the United States from France a couple of decades ago and have slowly but steadily grown in popularity since then. Originally designed in the eighteenth century for personal hygiene between weekly baths, bidets closely resemble toilets, but they require more complicated plumbing and cost more. Some bidets are fitted with a faucet that fills the bowl, the same way a sink is filled. In other models a vertical or horizontal spray issues a gentle shower of water, while still other units offer both of those options. Some newer fixtures combine the functions of a toilet and a bidet in one unit.

Bidets require a hot-and-cold supply line, a drain, and about 8 square feet of space. They are produced by all major manufacturers in the same colors and styles as other bathroom fixtures, whether traditional or contemporary. Prices range from about $300 to perhaps $1,000 for colors or special finishes, such as stainless steel.

Brass

Chrome

Brass and Chrome

Oil-Rubbed Bronze

Brushed Nickel

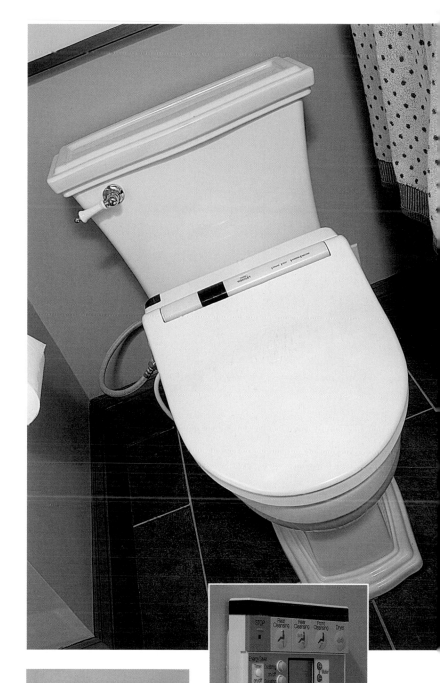

ABOVE LEFT AND RIGHT This bidet and toilet are a matched set. For a custom look, coodinate toilet-seat hinges (above) with other hardware.

ABOVE FAR RIGHT A technologically advanced toilet, this fixture also works as a bidet, incorporating a warm-water personal cleansing system into the seat.

RIGHT AND FAR RIGHT The touch-control panel lets you adjust washing and drying. Some systems come with a remote control.

5

Vanity Flair

What is one of the blessings of bigger bathrooms? There's finally room for plentiful storage—and so many efficient and interesting ways to supply it. The tried-and-true vanity is still around, but there are also storage pieces that mimic antiques and bathroom "furniture" that provides places for absolutely everything. Even medicine cabinets have evolved into important design elements. For inspiration, study the photographs on the following pages where you'll find the latest looks. You can also read up on the trends and improvements that can organize your bathroom and make your life easier.

- vanities
- cabinet construction
- define your style
- cabinet finishes
- bathroom furniture
- medicine cabinets

Thanks to a white-tile toe kick that acts as a continuation of the floor, this vanity looks like it's floating, which complements the room's light and airy tone.

Go Green

Look for a custom-cabinetry company that uses wood certified by the Forest Stewardship Council (FSC).

the design attention that has been focused on the bathroom for several decades has improved every aspect of it. The vanity still reigns as the major supplier of storage, but these days it looks better, stores more, and has grown taller. Because one height does not suit all people, stock vanities now range from the standard 30 inches to 36 inches high, which is easier on the back for tall people. With two vanities in the master bath, each one can be tailored to a comfortable height for its user. Vanities are also available in a couple of depths these days—18-inch-deep units free up floor space; 24-inch-deep models store more. To further improve the storage picture, the vanity is often supplemented by additional cabinets, open shelves, and freestanding furniture. Even the medicine cabinet has increased in size, functionality, and good looks.

Learn some cabinet lingo before you go shopping. For example, stock vanity cabinets, your least-expensive option, are preassembled, factory-made units that you can often take home the same day. Some of them are well made and attractive, but sizes, styles, and finishes are limited. You'll pay a little more for a semicustom design because the variety of finishes and styles is greater, but these units are also factory made and available only in standard sizes. Custom cabinets, the most pricey option, offer the greatest design leeway because they are built to your specifications.

vanities

Available at home centers and large retail stores, stock cabinets can be inexpensive, as low as about $100 for a 36-inch-wide model. Check construction carefully before you buy—not all of them are well made. A 36-inch-wide semicustom vanity, generally available through cabinet showrooms, will cost about $300. Custom units, which are available through some manufacturers or local cabinetmakers, can be costly, but you will get a well-made product that meets specific needs.

OPPOSITE AND LEFT
Vanity cabinets come in many styles, from traditional (opposite) to Modern (left). For something unique, order a custom design.

OPPOSITE Consider using tile in unusual places. Here, cabinets inlaid with an intricate tile pattern create an interesting design element.

RIGHT Although a floating sink alone would have worked in this minimalist bathroom, a wall-mounted cabinet adds warmth while hiding the plumbing.

vanity and cabinet dimensions

STOCK BATHROOM CABINET DIMENSIONS (based on standard sizes in inches)

Cabinet	Width	Height	Depth
Sink base	15-72	28-36	16-21
Drawer base	12–21	31½-34½	21-24
Tall linen cabinet	9-24	83-96	21
Vanity linen cabinet	9-18	48-83	21
Vanity hamper cabinet	15-18	31½-33½	21

stow in style

Floating cabinets create a storage opportunity underneath where neatly folded towels become a design element.

ABOVE LEFT Dark wood cabinets are striking against the neutral walls and floor. Dark-stained wood adds a formal elegance to the room.

ABOVE RIGHT Although boxy vanities are the norm, they certainly aren't a requirement. Play around with different shapes and lines to find what suits the space.

OPPOSITE Identical vanities, positioned about 1 ft. apart, create a pleasing symmetry in the room while providing two people with space and personal storage all their own.

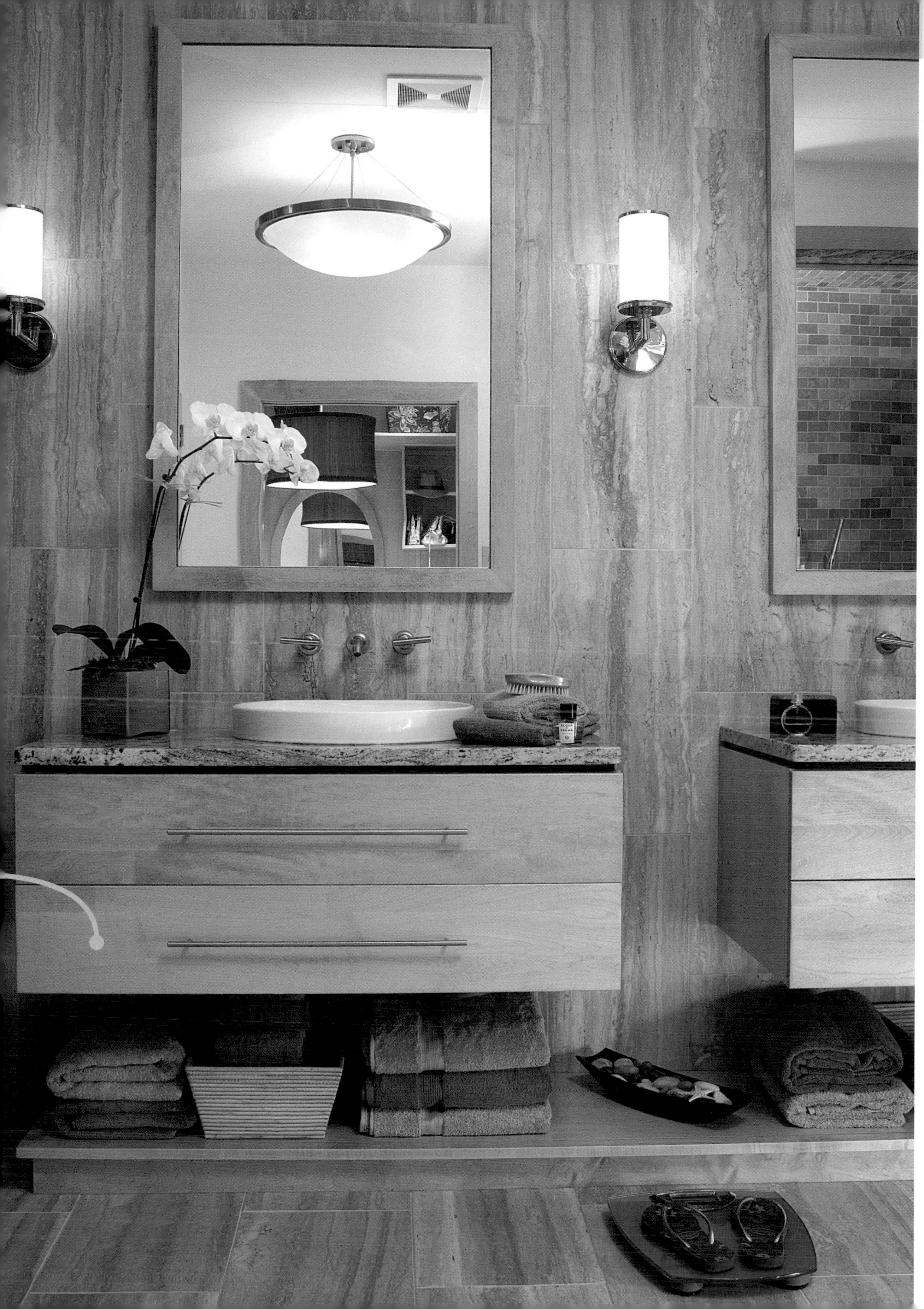

ABOVE The beauty of this vanity area lies in the details, such as the cut-glass design on the mirrors and the trimwork.

BELOW LEFT A furniture-like vanity seems to enlarge this diminutive space.

BELOW RIGHT The paneled drawers echo the bathtub surround.

cabinet construction

his is the day of the discount when it comes to home-improvement products. The rock-bottom prices you see advertised sometimes may be tempting, but protect yourself from vanity "lemons" by checking cabinet quality carefully before you buy. Beware of drawers that fail to open smoothly and are held together with nails, glue, or staples. Look for interiors that are finished, including rear surfaces. If there are shelves in the vanities you like, be sure they are adjustable—another sign of quality—and that they measure ⅝-inch thick to prevent bowing. Fine solid-wood cabinets and sturdy plywood cases with solid-wood doors will withstand daily wear and tear and damage from the bathroom's moist, steamy environment. However, particleboard or laminates over particleboard do not stand up as well and may quickly warp, peel, or cup when exposed to a great deal of moisture. For help selecting a vanity countertop material, refer to Chapter 3, "The Surfaces," beginning on page 56.

Typical of the good-looking and generously sized bathroom vanity of today, this double-size vanity cabinet offers an abundance of drawer and behind-door storage for a master retreat.

LEFT If you like the look of furniture in the bath, several manufacturers now carry items that resemble fine antique dressers. If you already have a piece you like, you may be able to retrofit it with plumbing.

ABOVE An above-counter lav and backsplash-mounted fittings are unobtrusive and consistent with the overall simplicity of this vanity, which resembles an antique wash-stand.

furniture-style vanities

A couple of years ago, somebody—an enterprising home-owner, perhaps, or an imaginative interior designer—came upon the idea of converting an antique washstand into a bathroom vanity, complete with a sink and all the necessary plumbing. The idea spread quickly, as most good ideas do, and soon many homeowners were asking their designers and remodeling contractors to help them duplicate this look. These furniture-like vanities not only added eccentric charm and relieved the monotony of banks of cabinets that all looked alike, but actually provided more storage in some cases. It wasn't long before cabinet manufacturers jumped on the bandwagon and began infusing their bath collections

with trendy new vanities crafted, glazed, distressed, and ornamented with classic architectural trim to look like antique wash stands, chests of drawers, and tables.

Taking the idea a little bit further, cabinet companies have now added armoires, mirrors, wall cabinets, shelves, and other storage pieces to their lines and designed them to harmonize with their furniture-like vanities. The bathroom furniture trend began with retrofitted antiques, but now that it has taken hold so firmly, contemporary-looking pieces—streamlined console tables, sleek bureaus, etc.—are also available for homeowners with a preference for modern design.

framed versus frameless designs

In framed construction, a rectangular frame outlines the cabinet box to add strength and provide a place to attach the door. The doors on frameless cabinets are laid flush over the box. No frame is visible, and hinges are often invisible as well.

Frameless A European concept that took hold here in the 1960s, frameless cabinets are a standby in contemporary-style bathrooms. The doors fit over the entire cabinet box for a sleek and streamlined look.

Framed Cabinets with a visible frame offer richness of detail that is appropriate for traditional and country-style bathrooms and their many design cousins.

the rooms of your home display a certain style, one that reflects your tastes and personality. Why should the bathroom be any different? No longer a bland and lackluster room, it's as valid a place as any to express your decorating sensibility. And the best place to start is with the vanity and other cabinets. They will establish the overall style, which you can reinforce with fixtures, fittings, surfaces, and accessories.

Is a casual country look your cup of tea? You might begin with pine cabinets in a light stain or a slightly distressed, painted finish. White-painted, bead-board cabinets also impart a country flavor. A traditionally styled bathroom would look slightly more formal. For the vanity, you might choose rich medium- or dark-toned wood enlivened with brass hardware and some fine-furniture details, such as raised panels, rope trim, or applied molding. To create a contemporary bath you'd select clean-lined cabinets fin-

define your style

ished in laminate, metal, or light-toned woods, such as ash or birch, with minimal hardware. For a period-style, such as a Victorian bath, dark, ornately carved wood is one way to go; a lighter Victorian look would feature a white painted wood cabinet with simple detailing and a marble top. To help you achieve your design dreams, cabinet manufacturers sell all of the vanities described here and more, but you can also create a one-of-a-kind look by converting a piece of furniture or going the custom route.

OPPOSITE TOP A unique imported cabinet completes the elegant look of this Asian-inspired bathroom.

OPPOSITE BOTTOM LEFT The style of this modern bath design is characterized by clean lines and symmetry.

OPPOSITE BOTTOM RIGHT Warm wood cabinets and complementary cream countertops are a graceful combination.

RIGHT New custom-made traditional-style cabinetry with an antique, off-white finish also has elegant furniture-like details, such as recessed-panel doors, vanity legs, fluting, and carved rosettes.

cabinet door style choices

Door styles are strictly decorative. Styles pictured, left to right: reveal-overlay panel; frame and panel; flat panel; beaded frame and panel; square raised panel; curved raised panel; bead-board panel; and cathedral panel.

bath storage has never been more appealing

BELOW This bathroom is a true expression of its owner; the design features a unique island vanity made of wood, stone, and metal, with storage underneath.

BELOW RIGHT A lighted soffit above the vanity, elegant cornicing and fluted side panels, and a warm green finish create a more personal look to this traditional-style piece.

OPPOSITE The vanity, with simple modern lines and solid color, anchors the room among its various patterns.

and tailored to individual needs

highs 'n lows

New vanity sizes accommodate people of different heights— no more deep bending to wash your face.

Go Green

Consider using low-VOC (volatile organic compound) wood finishes, such as linseed oil or beeswax.

bathroom furniture

furniture-like vanities have been such a big hit with homeowners that they have given rise to another trend—bathroom "furniture." Now, instead of restricting themselves to a single, unique-looking vanity that resembles a piece of furniture, designers are outfitting baths with several freestanding pieces, all of which look like they have been imported from the bedroom, living room, or even the kitchen. Because new bathrooms, especially master baths, tend to be large today, they can accommodate similarly scaled pieces such as bureaus, sideboards, and armoires. Besides, furniture introduces a degree of warmth and coziness not typically found in the bathroom. You can implement the look in your own bath by importing pieces from other rooms in your house or by scouring flea markets and antique stores to find a few likely candidates. If those shopping jaunts seem like too much of an effort, you can turn to cabinet manufacturers, many of whom have recently introduced custom-made, furniture-quality bath cabinets into their lines. And you'll be glad to know that this new design approach has done more than beautify the bathroom—it has also improved storage capacity. A 6-foot-tall armoire will look fabulous and will hold more items than a standard cabinet; as will the new bureau-like vanities, with their drawers of various sizes and shapes.

OPPOSITE An artful above-counter lav and wall-mounted fixtures camouflage the utility of this elegant vanity, which looks like fine furniture.

BELOW A sizeable his-and-her arrangement eases congestion at busy times of the day. Fabric-lined glass-paneled cabinets hide clutter and add design interest.

LEFT A hutch designed with drawers for linens and shelves for toiletries is a perfect addition to the bathroom, with attractive storage for all of its incidentals.

BELOW LEFT Storage doesn't have to be all drawers and cupboards. Manufacturers offer a wide range of clever solutions, such as this hidden hamper.

BELOW RIGHT Above-counter lavs and wall-mounted fixtures in the same finish as the mirrors create a cohesive look in this large space.

OPPOSITE This design incorporates niche storage for those little everyday essentials.

steal storage solutions from other rooms

smart storage

Taking its cue from the kitchen, this cabinet ensemble maximizes storage for the bath with drawers and cupboards in handy sizes.

open shelving

In the bathroom, you don't have to stow all your stuff behind closed doors. In fact, it's convenient to have some items, such as towels and soaps, up for grabs when you need them. That's where open shelves come in handy. They're economical, practical, and if used imaginatively to show off pretty perfume bottles, graceful jars of lotions, or stacks of colorful towels, they can be decorative, too.

The flexibility of open shelves lets you use every square inch of the bath to create new storage, including places that a standard cabinet won't fit. For example, convert the space between wall studs into shallow sets of shelves for toiletries and small bottles. Nooks such as these can be created anywhere in the room, but they are particularly handy near the sink. Install a couple of shelves above the tub for extra towels. To compensate for the lack of a vanity, put a little shelf above a pedestal sink. Go to it—the possibilities are practically endless.

BELOW LEFT A large cabinet would look out of place in this minimalist bathroom. Open shelving provides a place for exactly what is needed in an unobtrusive way.

BELOW Open shelving makes practical use of space here. The bright red towels in this niche are functional while providing an additional pop of color.

OPPOSITE While open shelving can be attractive, closed cabinets, recessed medicine cabinets behind mirrors, and a hidden wall niche hold all of the everyday toiletries that would clutter a countertop.

ordinary things can be beautiful when displayed

6

Light and Air

In today's bigger, more beautiful baths, lighting is more important than ever. For the small unimaginative bathrooms of days gone by, a ceiling light and maybe a fixture over the sink were enough to do the job. But today, bath designers and other experts recommend a layered approach to lighting. Start with some daylight via windows or skylights that open to provide ventilation as well as light. Then add a dose of pleasant artificial light that enhances the sunshine and illuminates the whole room at night. Don't forget: you'll need task lights for efficiency and safety in bathing and grooming areas.

- **natural light**
- **artificial lighting**
- **ventilation**

The large mirror above this vanity area helps reflect the natural light that cascades through the picture window.

natural light

remodeling a bathroom often includes removing the small original windows and opening up the space with larger windows. Or you can add a skylight to flood the area with natural light without worrying about privacy issues or using up valuable wall space in a small room.

Whether you are remodeling an old bath or building a new one, pay attention to the variety of options you have for incorporating windows. You will want to get one that looks best with the rest of the room, of course, but don't forget to consider energy efficiency. Today's windows and skylights are better sealed than those produced in the past. Construction is tighter, so there is reduced air infiltration around the frames. Multiple panes, improved coatings, and gas-filled spaces between panes can reduce both heat loss and unwanted heat gain. Some coatings filter out ultraviolet rays. When shopping, always consider your climate and the window's orientation.

ABOVE These top-down, bottom-up cellular shades are cordless, maintaining the clean lines of the Asian-inspired design of the room.

LEFT Sunlight streams into this shower space, creating the sense of being outdoors.

OPPOSITE Large picture windows give this bath an indoor-outdoor feeling.

open up your new bath with larger windows

window types

Windows can be fixed (meaning you can't open them) **or operable.** Glass block is an example of a fixed window, but even clear-glass framed panels can be fixed. These windows let in light and views, but they don't admit air. Examples of operable window types include double- and single-hung windows.

- **Double-hung windows** have both an upper and lower sash that ride up and down in their own channels.

- **Single-hung windows** are like double-hung units except that only their lower sash moves.

- **Casement windows** are hinged vertically to swing in or out. You can operate them with a crank.

- **Sliding windows** have top and bottom tracks on which the sash move sideways.

- **Awning windows** are hinged horizontally to swing in or out.

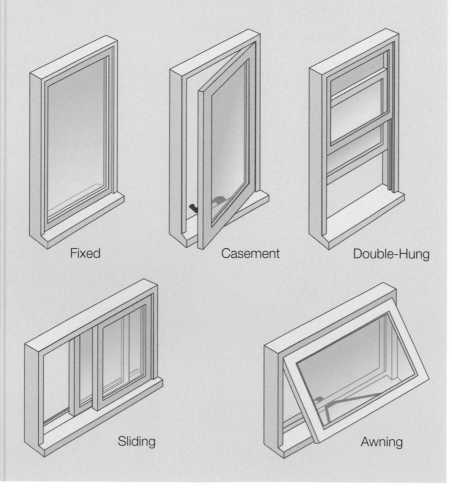

Fixed   Casement   Double-Hung

Sliding   Awning

LEFT A large, round window with a spoked grille transformed a dark bath alcove into the sunny focal point of the room.

BELOW LEFT A transom window offers ample natural light without compromising privacy.

RIGHT Double-hung windows with muntins suit the traditional architecture of this room.

BELOW RIGHT Casement windows are easy to operate. Depending on how they are hinged, they can swing out or into the room.

Go Green

Abundant natural light is the most beautiful—and eco-friendly—enhancement to your bathroom.

skylights and roof windows

If you don't have access to a window, investigate a vented skylight or a roof window. Skylights supply up to 30 percent more light than vertical windows, and they also make the room feel larger. In a house with an attic, you can even install a shaft or tunnel that makes it possible to bring light and air from an operable skylight or roof window into a bathroom. Best of all, many of the newer models work by remote control for maximum convenience and ease of operation.

OPPOSITE Artificial and natural light strike a perfect balance in this luxurious bathroom.

BELOW The sloped ceiling over twin lavs is an ideal location for a skylight.

RIGHT Pouring in through multiple windows and a solar tunnel in the ceiling, sunshine brightens this tub area, inviting a long, relaxing soak.

solar tunnel

A solar tunnel lets you enjoy the benefits of a skylight without installing a standard-size skylight shaft.

artificial lighting

good lighting provides adequate illumination and enhances the look and feeling of the space it brightens. It also increases safety. There are several types of artificial lighting. It's wise to include all of them in your plans for a new bath. The first, *ambient lighting,* is the general illumination that is required for any room. The optimum number and location of general light sources (fixtures) depends upon the size of the room. The second type, task lighting, is what you need for grooming. To look good in the mirror, *task lighting* should come at you from both sides, radiating from the middle of your face (about 60 to 66 inches from the floor for most adults). Avoid lighting the vanity area from above, which will cause shadows. The third type, *accent lighting,* isn't necessary in a bathroom, but it can add a decorative touch. Small strip lights or compact spotlights mounted inside a glass-door cabinet, under the mirror, beneath a raised tub, or recessed into a soffit above the vanity are excellent examples. They don't give off a lot of light, just enough to create a mood.

OPPOSITE TOP Recessed fixtures create good general lighting throughout this space.

OPPOSITE BOTTOM LEFT These delicate, jewel-like pendants are excellent for accent lighting.

OPPOSITE BOTTOM RIGHT Diffused side lights provide illumination for grooming at the lav.

ABOVE Opaque shades force the light up and down for a flattering, no-glare effect.

how much do you need?

In all but the tiniest of bathrooms, ceiling-mounted lamps are necessary for sufficient general illumination. A good choice is recessed lighting. How much you need, of course, depends on the size of the room. If the bathroom is less than 100 sq. ft., one fixture is sufficient. Add another fixture for each additional 50 sq. ft. If the surfaces around the room are light-absorbing dark hues, such as mahogany-stained cabinets, deep-colored walls, or black granite countertops, you may have to compensate with stronger lamps. If the bulbs you are using are not providing enough general light, you need to substitute them with ones that have more lumens, not with higher-wattage bulbs. The next time you shop for bulbs, read the packaging, which indicates the lumens per watt (LPW) produced by a bulb.

dimmers

Install dimmers on the lights so that all members of the household can adjust light levels to meet their own needs.

OPPOSITE Colorful twin pendant lamps cast light down and to the side of the lav to reduce shadows.

LEFT These sconces aim the light upward for a glare-free environment.

BELOW LEFT Downward-facing sconces may produce some glare, but that can be minimized with shades.

BELOW Compact side lights are excellent light sources for applying makeup or shaving.

LEFT Eyeball spotlights recessed into the soffit area over the vanity should be directed to the side.

BELOW LEFT Sconces on either side of a mirror cast shadow-free light.

BELOW RIGHT In a small room, the vanity light may provide general illumination, too.

OPPOSITE TOP Some medicine cabinets come with built-in lighting, which is usually fluorescent.

OPPOSITE BOTTOM These light fixtures can accommodate either fluorescent or incandescent bulbs.

lighting for mirrors

You'll need even, shadow-free lighting for applying makeup, shaving, or caring for hair. It should illuminate both sides of the face, under the chin, and the top of the head. Plan to use at least 120 incandescent watts. Never aim lighting into the mirror. Decorative sconces installed on either side of a small mirror at face height do the job nicely. Place them no higher than 60 in. above the floor and at least 28 in. but not more than 60 in. apart, unless you pair them with another vanity light source.

If fluorescent side lights are mandated by your local code, use the deluxe warm-white fluorescent bulbs that more closely resemble natural light. Install them up to 48 in. apart for sufficient lighting and supplement them with recessed or surface-mounted ceiling fixtures. A large mirror used over a double vanity will require a different approach: treat each lav as a separate task area and light each one.

lighting for tubs and showers

Light around the tub and shower area has to be bright enough for safety and grooming, adjusting water temperature or showerheads, and reading (if you care to read while you soak in the tub). Recessed downlights or any other fixtures designed for wet areas are fine. Shielded fixtures eliminate glare, and shatter-resistant white acrylic diffusers are the safest. Any light fixture installed in a wet or damp area has to be protected properly so that water cannot accumulate in wiring compartments, lamp holders, or other electrical parts. Your professional electrician will know how to handle the situation and can recommend the proper light fixture.

ABOVE LEFT Here, simple Roman shades roll down for privacy, and recessed lights illuminate the bath.

ABOVE RIGHT A large window, a chandelier, and cove lighting brighten the area around this tub.

LEFT Bright white light from recessed fixtures washes the wall around this tub and dramatizes the glass-tile design.

OPPOSITE A single fixture—rated for a moist area—is all that is needed here.

light fantastic

Both natural and artificial lighting are key components to any bath design, so never skimp on your lighting budget.

ABOVE LEFT Incandescent bulbs with fabric shades offer warm, flattering illumination with a slightly pink cast.

LEFT Built-in fluorescent lighting on each side of this mirror produces a whiter, truer tone.

RIGHT Low-voltage halogen lamps bedecked with crystal-bead "curtains" bedazzle in this powder room.

improved bulbs

types of bulbs

Here's a description of the most common types of bulbs and their advantages and disadvantages.

Incandescent. Like sunlight, incandescent bulbs emit "continuous-spectrum light," or light that contains every color. Illumination from these bulbs, in fact, is even warmer than sunlight, making its effect very appealing in a room. It makes our skin tones look good and even enhances our feeling of well-being. The drawbacks to incandescent bulbs are that they use a lot of electricity and produce a lot of heat. However, they come in a variety of shapes, sizes, and applications. (One type features a waterproof lens cover that makes it suitable for over a tub or inside of a shower.) These bulbs can be clear, diffuse, tinted, or colored, and they may have a reflective coating inside.

Fluorescent. These energy-efficient bulbs cast a diffuse, shadowless light that makes them great for general illumination. They are very energy efficient, but the old standard fluorescents are quite unflattering, making everything and everyone appear bluish and bland. Newer warm-white fluorescent bulbs render color in a way that more closely resembles sunlight. Fluorescents are available both in the familiar tube versions and in compact styles. In some parts of the country, local codes require fluorescent lights to conform to energy conservation mandates.

Halogen. This is actually a type of incandescent lamp that operates at greater energy efficiency. It produces brighter, whiter light at a lower wattage. One disadvantage is a higher price tag. However, although halogens cost more up front, they last longer than conventional incandescents. Because a halogen bulb produces a higher heat output than other incandescents, it requires a special shielding. The low-voltage version of halogen bulbs produces a 50 percent brighter light than standard halogen bulbs. These are compact and use less electricity, which makes them more energy efficient, too.

Xenon. Like halogens, xenon bulbs—frequently used in auto headlights—can be compact and produce a bright, white light that is very true to sunlight. But unlike halogens, which produce a lot of heat and emit harmful ultraviolet (UV) rays, xenon bulbs have low-heat output, making them more energy efficient.

render better light

OPPOSITE Vertical Hollywood-style strip lights with a diffuser project a flattering ambiance.

ABOVE A rectangular pendant over the lav has a modern look that makes an interesting pairing with the artful antler chandelier.

LEFT Moorish-style lamps enhance this Mediterranean-inspired design.

lighting fixtures can reinforce a decorating style

Go Green

**Compact fluores-
cent bulbs use
about 75 percent
less energy and
last about 20
times as long as
standard bulbs.**

ABOVE The polished finish on this high-quality sconce can withstand moist conditions in the bath.

ABOVE RIGHT A specialty light fixture transforms the bath into an elegant, private haven.

RIGHT A brushed-nickel finish matches the rest of the room's hardware.

OPPOSITE TOP A linear sconce is an alternative to a light strip.

OPPOSITE BOTTOM A frosted shade softens the light.

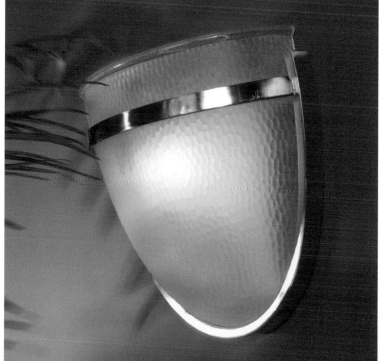

RIGHT While most windows provide ventilation, an Energy Star-rated exhaust fan is more effective.

BELOW To effectively remove moisture from the bathroom, match the fan's capacity to the room's dimensions.

OPPOSITE The bathroom must be well-ventilated because the moisture generated there can lead to mold and mildew.

a dequate ventilation is a must in any humid environment, and you can't get much more humid than the modern bathroom retreat. Those fabulous home-spa features use more water than standard fixtures, raising the humidity level in the bathroom accordingly. The only solution is a good ventilation system. Ventilation combats the steam and condensation that causes mildew, rot, and deterioration of the bathroom's surfaces and the surrounding rooms or exterior walls of the house. If you haven't installed a proper moisture barrier between the bathroom and the exterior wall, you

ventilation

may face serious structural damage in addition to peeling and chipping paint. If you install glossy ceramic, stone, or glass tiles on bathroom surfaces, your ventilation needs are greater than if you installed an absorbent material, such as cork. (Unfortunately, many absorbent materials aren't appropriate for the bathroom because they can decay and spread bacteria.) Even glossy paints can resist absorption and create problems with mold and mildew. Beyond concerns for bathroom surfaces and structural elements, imagine the air quality in a stuffy and unventilated bathroom. Noxious fumes released into the air by cleaning solutions and grooming products, including hair spray and nail polish, pose a health risk. The most common side effects of this indoor air pollution include eye, nose, and throat irritation. Not exactly the kind of picture you had in mind when you dreamed of creating a relaxing, sybaritic haven in your new bathroom.

7

Get Stylish

Some time ago people said goodbye to the boring "necessary" room and happily greeted the bath of the twenty-first century, with its limitless opportunities for comfort, design, and personal expression. Restricted only by the size of their bathrooms—and the size of their budgets—homeowners are eagerly accepting these design opportunities. Whether your decorating style preferences run to traditional, nostalgic, high tech, or drop-dead glamorous, you'll find ideas for bringing them to life in your new bath with color and other special details in the pages that follow.

- **color**
- **trimwork and paneling**
- **window treatments**
- **style specifics**

Red accents make this room an energizing and fresh area to prepare for your day.

color is probably your greatest decorating tool. Don't be afraid of it—it also happens to be one of the easiest things to change. So why do people typically stick with a neutral palette in the bathroom? A dated color on a permanent fixture can be expensive to change because usually you have to replace the fixture. However, special new paints make

color

it possible to refurbish ceramic and porcelain with a new color for a fraction of the cost of replacement.

If you still want to stick with white or beige for the tub, sink, and toilet, introduce color to the walls or with accessories. Just pick up a can of paint and see how color can transform the space in no time at all. If you don't like what you've done, just grab another can of paint and start again. It's inexpensive and easy to apply.

One of the simplest things that you can do to test out a color is to apply it to a sheet of white poster board, hang it on the wall, and live with it a few days. Look at it during the day; then wait for evening and look at it again under varying levels of artificial light. Is the color still appealing to you? What effect does it have on the space at different times of the day? Even if you're thinking about tiling a wall or installing wallpaper, pick out the dominant color; find a matching paint; and apply this simple test.

OPPOSITE White furniture and fixtures are made visually interesting with stone, paint, and tiles.

ABOVE LEFT This unexpected shade of green is balanced by neutral colors elsewhere in the room.

LEFT The mosaic-tile backsplash accentuates the paint and accessories' gold and honey hues.

ABOVE RIGHT Bright natural light floods this open space with energy and warmth, perfect for early mornings.

RIGHT Life's a day at the beach here, where blue hues and beach-themed decor complement the white paneling.

OPPOSITE French reproduction wallpaper features a classic motif. The bold color dramatizes this pretty powder room.

BELOW RIGHT A minimal, but not boring, color palette of warm chocolate and cream hues sets the stage for this bathroom's updated cottage style.

paint and wallpaper

While you're thinking about color for the new bathroom, consider the types of paint, wallpaper, and fabric to use. Remember, bathrooms have lots of glossy surfaces, which reflect light. Unless you want an intense effect, use low-luster paints and matte finishes.

If you are concerned about moisture, especially in a room without ducted ventilation, shop for products that have been treated with mildewcide in the manufacturing process. Bathrooms are perfect breeding grounds for mold. When moisture seeps behind wallpaper, it creates a moldy, peeling mess. Luckily, this is a problem that can be avoided because there is a wide selection of products and glues that are designed specifically for bathroom applications.

Go Green

New environmentally friendly paints have low- or zero-VOCs, which are better for the air both inside and outside your home.

ABOVE Patterns in bathrooms can range from whimsical to subdued. This quirky aquatic wallpaper mates with an elaborate seashell mirror to tie together the theme.

RIGHT This bathroom's curvilinear theme can be seen in every aspect of its decorating, from the patterned toile wallpaper to the curved details in the sink, lights, and even toilet.

OPPOSITE The stripes in this bath are balanced by angular, understated furniture and fixtures. The stone floor and countertop give the room a sophisticated feel.

choosing patterns

After you've settled on a color scheme, you can look for wallpaper and fabrics to carry through your theme. Two major factors in deciding which patterns to choose are the location and size of the room. Look at the adjoining areas, especially the ones that you must pass through to get to the bathroom. Think of them sequentially. If you want stripes in the bath but the adjoining hallway has a floral wallpaper, match the colors. In a small bathroom, a bold print may be too busy. On the other hand, it may be just what is needed to make an extra-large space feel cozy. Vertical designs will add height to a room. Conversely, horizontal motifs will draw the eye around it. In general, patterned wallpaper looks best in a traditional-style decor. In a contemporary scheme, subtle patterns that don't detract from the architecture and the materials are best. And avoid trendy looks unless you want to make changes every couple of years.

paint or paper

Too busy to paint special effects? Not to worry— shop for a wallpaper that mimics the look.

It's an avant-garde look for a traditional home, but the hand-painted walls in this tiny space express the homeowners' artful originality.

give the room some personality

Whether you are decorating the bathroom of your master suite or a powder room, there is plenty of leeway for personalizing the space and making it truly your own. Consider your taste: perhaps you are drawn to the rich hues of Mediterranean style, such as in the room below right. There's no reason that even a smaller room can't be a part of a more elaborate theme. Your decorating can extend to the nooks and crannies, or you can take a more simplistic approach, as seen in the photo below left. Leave boring bathrooms for other people!

- **Show it off.** Small nooks can be great for displaying collections or beautiful items.

- **Light it up.** Think about how lighting can add to the theme of your room, in addition to where function calls for it.

- **Share it with others.** Consider guests' needs, and what items are best to keep visible and accessible.

- **Keep it current.** Don't forget to update your bath with new items to keep it current, interesting, and enjoyable.

painting stripes

Stripes are among the most attractive painted effects you can add to a surface. Alternating broad and thin stripes, such as the ones used in the bathrooom opposite top left, can go on fairly quickly and evenly. If your hand isn't particularly steady, you may want to roll on the paint rather than use a brush to apply it. You can find narrow rollers in paint and craft shops, or you can cut down a standard-size roller to the desired width of the stripe. It's best to use a thick paint because you have to make one uninterrupted pass with the roller. Avoid running the roller up and down.

Load the roller from a paint tray. Start at the top, and run the roller straight down (or across) the surface. For a neat look, mask the edges before applying the paint.

OPPOSITE Large spaces can accomodate bold patterns. Earth tones throughout this bath keep the surfaces and patterns tied together and harmonious.

ABOVE LEFT The beautiful green and brown shades of this garden theme are accentuated by stripes and waves reminiscent of grass, plant stalks, and trees.

ABOVE RIGHT Horizontal stripes made of glass-tile strips draw the eye around this bath. Sand-colored surfaces and fixtures create a calm, Zen-like atmosphere.

RIGHT Not all lines need to be arrow-straight to be fashionable. Curlicues in the walpaper add a graceful and elegant touch to this bathroom's walls.

classic columns

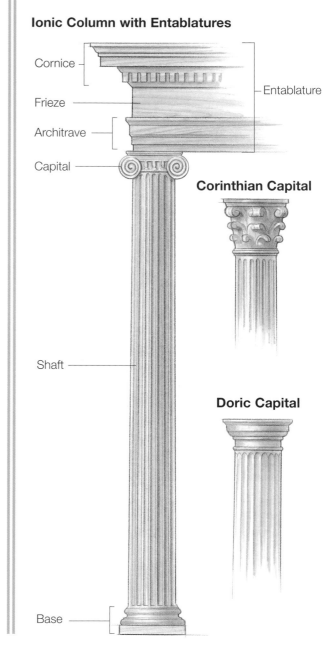

Ionic Column with Entablatures

Cornice

Frieze

Architrave

Capital

Entablature

Corinthian Capital

Shaft

Doric Capital

Base

TOP White painted columns and paneling make the tub area the focal point in this bathroom.

LEFT Here, columns help to define separate spaces, but they are stained to match the rest of the wood for a cohesive look.

Pilaster Construction

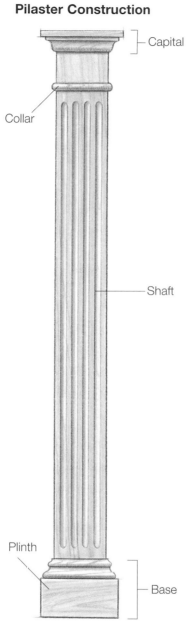

Capital

Collar

Shaft

Plinth

Base

Columns can also be made of fiberglass, which is lightweight, or concrete, and then finished with paint or plaster for a stone-like appearance.

door and window casings

Bellyband Casing with Rosette

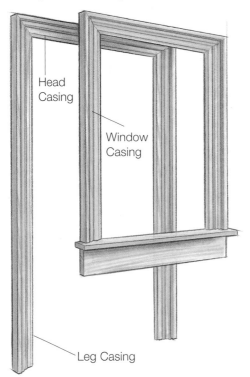

Head Casing

Window Casing

Leg Casing

Bellyband Casing with Rosette

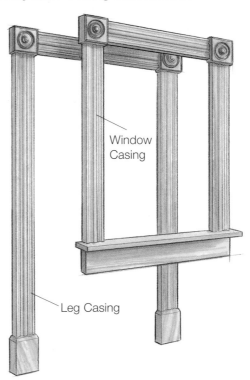

Window Casing

Leg Casing

Arts and Crafts–Style Casing

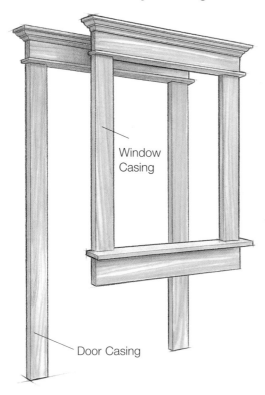

Window Casing

Door Casing

Fluted Casings with Decorative Head

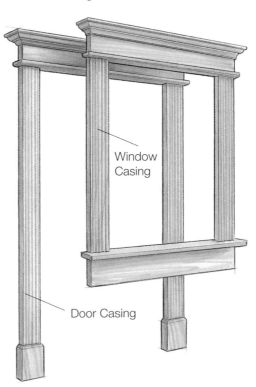

Window Casing

Door Casing

ABOVE These windows and the French door feature Victorian-style mitered window casings.

ABOVE RIGHT The plain casings reinforce the simplicity of this Arts and Crafts-style design.

RIGHT You can see how the right trim ehances this window's shape.

Choose a window treatment and control system that will both enhance your comfort while in the bathroom and help create the design expression that you are seeking. You can take your first cue from the climate where you live. In a hot climate, window treatments should block heavy direct sunlight, especially if the room faces south or west. In a cool climate, you'll need insulated window treatments to block drafts during the winter, especially if the bathroom faces north. Next consider privacy. If your bath window is visible from the yard or neighboring house, choose a device that can be easily closed to block all views to the interior. Your final selection will have to accommodate the type and size of your windows, the appearance you want, and your budget. Of course, for the bath, it's always best to choose easy-clean materials.

window treatments

OPPOSITE When privacy control is important, blinds are a practical option. The custom-made units here have been fabricated in wood to match the room.

BELOW Is there ever a reason to let a window remain undressed? Absolutely! In this case, privacy isn't a concern, and so this powder room's pretty oval-shape window can remain on view.

pretty shape

Some windows are almost purely for decoration— they admit light, but you can't open them.

window treatments add a finishing touch

OPPOSITE Woven shades in a deep chocolate brown that matches the wood provide privacy without totally blocking sunlight.

LEFT An appealing yellow-and-red toile shade bordered in red and white plaid adds color and pattern to a white powder room.

BELOW LEFT Full-length shutters on tall windows can be easily opened to admit light or closed for privacy.

BELOW A simple café curtain installed to cover three quarters of this window hangs from rings that glide across the tension rod with ease.

LEFT Raised-panel cabinets, crown molding, and shapely arched faucets in a satin-nickel finish come together to create an updated traditional look in this room.

BELOW Multicolor green tiles, wicker, and a faux-finished metal vanity have a natural feel.

OPPOSITE TOP With full access to a private outdoor area, this design has Zen appeal.

OPPOSITE BOTTOM Framless cabinets and a blend of rough-hewn stone and metal distinguish this rustic contemporary design.

the bath is a place where you can express your personal style. There are no rules, but styles do fall into several categories, one of which is sure to please you. In a contemporary bath, the mood is serene; fixtures, fittings, and cabinets are clean-lined and unembellished; and there is an emphasis on natural materials, such as stone, glass, and even metal. A traditional bath design relies on finely detailed cabinets in cherry or mahogany, rich, deep colors, and polished metal fittings to set a gracious and elegant tone. A country-style bath, often equipped with vintage-look tubs or pedestal lavs, is cheerier and more casual. Cottage country is casual, too, but a bit more subdued, focusing on soft pastels, faded fabrics, and gauzy curtains rather than the brighter colors of country. In both styles, however, white-painted or light cabinetry, distressed furniture, wicker pieces, baskets, and framed prints figure prominently. The key to Old World style is "old." All of the elements—mellow wood and rich shades of ochre, rust red, and olive green—should look like they've seen a lot of use but are not yet shabby. The new take on Victorian may include period-style fixtures and fittings, but the cabinets, surfaces, window treatments, and accessories will be less fussy than in the past.

style specifics

make a modern statement

ABOVE LEFT Today's contemporary design mixes interesting wood finishes and touches of stone. The bamboo vanity, slate flooring, and the tile border look organic here.

ABOVE RIGHT Glass is another key element in contemporary design. Here it is an unobtrusive partition that separates the shower from the tub.

OPPOSITE AND INSET Laminate cabinets are still popular with admirers of contemporary style. These have the clean, sleek lines that have traditionally defined the look, but the soft color adds personality. The "jet set" shower offers a number of relaxing options.

sparkle

Luminous glass tile isn't practical for an entire floor, but as an accent paired with stone or ceramic tile, it adds glamour.

OPPOSITE This elegant example of traditional style features classic details, such as the symmetrical arrangement of the vanities on each side of the tub.

OPPOSITE BOTTOM LEFT Gorgeous white marble with a beveled edge adds refinement.

OPPOSITE BOTTOM RIGHT In this detail of the bathroom you can see how modern fixtures can play off classic forms.

BELOW The rich, dark stain on the cabinetry recalls fine antique furniture. A pretty crystal chandelier adds a grace note.

Go Green

Want to keep the environment healthy the natural way? Add live plants, which can improve air quality and boost oxygen.

ABOVE RIGHT AND LEFT Long for Zen-like serenity? Bring elements of the outdoors inside your bath. Natural materials, such as the irregular-shaped stone used for the walls, look rustic yet refined here.

RIGHT The large tub overlooking the lake, made possible by glass walls, is the perfect way to get away from it all.

RIGHT Porcelain-tile walls and river rock on the shower floor create an outdoor feeling. Simple niches carved into the shower wall and finished with tiny glass tiles offer convenient nooks for neatly containing toiletries.

BELOW The extra-deep soaking tub is a welcome relief after a long day at the office or a work-out in the gym.

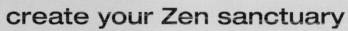

create your Zen sanctuary

immerse yourself in Old World tradition

OPPOSITE TOP   Oil-rubbed bronze sets off the fittings that sit atop the granite countertop.

OPPOSITE BOTTOM LEFT   An ornate iron chandelier evokes the formality of the room's design.

OPPOSITE BOTTOM RIGHT   Honey-stained cabinetry picks up color from the tiles and countertop.

ABOVE LEFT   Slate tile in various sizes and patterns was used to create the custom-built shower.

ABOVE RIGHT   The arched shape of the shower entrance elicits a sense of carved-stone doorways.

OPPOSITE Log beams, rustic cabinetry, richly veined marble, and an earthy-color wall are inviting elements in this design.

RIGHT Pine planks add a contemporary look to this room, as do the sleek brushed-chrome faucets with cross handles that serve the pair of above-counter lavs. A light-color stain keeps the overall look of the bathroom bright and cheery.

BELOW Exposed beams and a vaulted ceiling add drama to this updated version of cabin style. Modern lighting and a sleek vanity and faucets maintain the room's archtecturally clean lines.

a contemporary cabin

resource guide

manufacturers

Art & Maison

1852 NE 144th St.

North Miami, FL 33181

www.artandmaison.com

Manufactures Caemenstone® bath products.

Alchemy Glass

www.alchemy-glass.com

Manufactures glass sinks, countertops, mirrors and light fixtures.

American Standard

P.O. Box 6820

1 Centennial Plaza

Piscataway, NJ 08855

www.americanstandard-us.com

Manufactures plumbing and tile products.

Armstrong World Industries

2500 Columbia Ave.

P.O. Box 3001

Lancaster, PA 17604

717-397-0611

www.armstrong.com

Manufactures floors, cabinets, ceilings, and ceramic tile.

Artemide

www.artemide.com

Manufactures lighting fixtures.

Bach Faucets

19701 DaVinci

Lake Forest, CA 92610

866-863-6584

www.bachfaucet.com

Manufactures faucets.

Bemis Manufacturing Co.

300 Mill St.

P.O. Box 901

Sheboygan Falls, WI 53085

800-558-7651

www.bemismfg.com

Manufactures toilet seats.

Benjamin Moore

51 Chestnut Ridge Rd.

Montvale, NJ 07645

www.benjaminmoore.com

Manufactures paint.

CaesarStone USA

6840 Hayvenhurst Ave. Ste. 100

Van Nuys, CA 91406

818-779-0999

www.caesarstoneus.com

Manufactures quartz countertops.

The following list of manufacturers and associations is meant to be a general guide to additional industry and product-related sources. It is not intended as a listing of products and manufacturers represented by the photographs in this book.

Corian, a div. of DuPont

800-426-7426

www.corian.com

Manufactures solid surfacing.

Dex Studios

404-753-0600

www.dexstudios.com

Creates custom concrete sinks, tubs, and countertops.

Formica Corp.

10155 Reading Rd.

Cincinnati, OH 45241

513-786-3525

www.formica.com

Manufactures plastic laminate and solid surfacing.

Ginger

460-N Greenway Industrial Dr.

Fort Mill, SC 29708

www.gingerco.com

Manufactures lighting and bathroom accessories.

Herbeau Creations of America

3600 Westview Dr.

Naples, FL 34104

239-417-5368

www.herbeau.com

Makes vitreous china fixtures.

Hoesch Design

www.hoesch.de

Manufactures tubs and shower partitions.

Jaclo

129 Dermody St.

Cranford, NJ 07016

800-852-3906

www.jaclo.com

Manufactures showerheads and body sprays.

Jacuzzi Whirlpool Bath

2121N. California Blvd.

Walnut Creek, CA 94596

800-288-4002

www.jacuzzi.com

Manufactures jetted tubs and showers.

resource guide

Kohler

444 Highland Dr.

Kohler, WI 53044

800-456-4537

www.kohlerco.com

Manufactures plumbing products.

KraftMaid Cabinetry

P.O. Box 1055

15535 South State Ave.

Middlefield, OH 44062

440-632-5333

www.kraftmaid.com

Manufactures cabinetry.

Lightology

1718 West Fullerton Ave.

Chicago, IL 60614

866-954-4489

www.lightology.com

Manufactures lighting fixtures.

MGS Progetti

www.mgsprogetti.com

Manufactures stainless steel faucets.

Merillat

www.merillat.com

Manufactures cabinets.

Moen

25300 Al Moen Dr.

North Olmsted, OH 44070

800-289-6636

www.moen.com

Manufactures sinks and faucets.

Neo-Metro, a div. of Acorn Engineering Co.

P.O. Box 3527

City of Industry, CA 91744

800-591-9050

www.neo-metro.com

Manufactures countertops, tubs, lavs, and tile.

Neptune

www.bainsneptune.com

Manufactures bathtubs and showers.

NuTone, Inc.

4820 Red Bank Rd.

Cincinnati, OH 45227

888-336-3948

www.nutone.com

Manufactures ventilation fans, medicine cabinets, and lighting fixtures.

Price Pfister, Inc.

19701 Da Vinci

Foothill Ranch, CA 92610

800-732-8238

www.pricepfister.com

Manufactures faucets.

Rehau

www.rehau.co.uk

Manufactures under-floor heating systems.

Robern, a div. of Kohler

701 North Wilson Ave.

Bristol, PA 19007

215-826-9800

www.robern.com

Manufactures medicine cabinets and accessories.

Seagull Lighting Products, Inc.

301 West Washington St.

Riverside, NJ 08075

856-764-0500

www.seagulllighting.com

Manufactures lighting fixtures.

Schonbek Worldwide Lighting, Inc.

61 Industrial Ave.

Plattsburgh, NY 12901

800-836-1892

www.schonbek.com

Manufactures crystal lighting fixtures.

Sonia

www.sonia-sa.com

Manufactures bath fixtures.

Sonoma Cast Stone

P.O. Box 1721

Sonoma, CA 95476

888-807-4234

www.sonomastone.com

Makes custom concrete sinks and countertops.

Stone Forest

P.O. Box S. St. Francis Dr.

Santa Fe, NM 87501

888-682-2987

www.stoneforest.com

Makes metal and stone bathtubs and lavs.

resource guide

Toto USA

1155 Southern Rd.

Morrow, GA 30260

770-282-8686

www.totousa.com

Manufactures toilets, bidets, sinks, and bathtubs.

Velux-America

800-888-3589

www.velux.com

Manufactures skylights and solar tunnels.

Villeroy and Boch

3 South Middlesex Ave

Monroe Township, NJ 08831

877-505-5350

www.villeroy-boch.com

Manufactures fixtures, fittings, and furniture.

Waterworks

60 Backus Ave.

Danbury, CT 06810

800-998-2284

www.waterworks.com

Manufactures plumbing products.

Wetstyle

866-842-1367

www.wetstyle.ca

Manufactures bath fixtures.

Wilsonart International

P.O. Box 6110

Temple, TX 76503-6110

800-433-3222

www.wilsonart.com

Manufactures plastic laminate and solid surfacing.

Wood-Mode Fine Custom Cabinetry

1 Second St.

Kreamer, PA 17833

877-635-7500

www.wood-mode.com

Manufactures custom cabinetry.

Zodiaq, a div. of DuPont

www.zodiaq.com

800-426-7426

Manufactures quartz composite material.

associations

Ceramic Tile Institute of America (CTIOA)

12061 W. Jefferson Blvd.

Culver City, CA 90230-6219

310-574-7800

www.ctioa.org

A trade organization that promotes the ceramic tile industry. Its Web site provides consumer information about ceramic tile.

National Kitchen and Bath Association (NKBA)

687 Willow Grove St.

Hackettstown, NJ 07840

800-652-2776

www.nkba.org

A national trade organization for kitchen and bath professionals. It offers consumers product information and a referral service.

Tile Council of America, Inc.

100 Clemson Research Blvd.

Anderson, SC 29625

864-646-8453

www.tileusa.com

A trade organization dedicated to promoting the tile industry. It also provides consumer information on selecting and installing tile.

glossary

Absorption (light): The energy (wavelengths) not reflected by an object or substance. The color of a substance depends on the wavelength reflected.

Accent lighting: A type of light that highlights an area or object to emphasize that aspect of a room's character.

Accessible design: Design that accommodates persons with physical disabilities.

Accessories: Towel racks, soap dishes, and other items specifically designed for use in the bath.

Adaptable design: Design that can be easily changed to accommodate a person with disabilities.

Ambient light: General illumination that fills a room. There is no visible source of the light.

Antiscalding valve (pressure-balancing valve): A single-control fitting that contains a piston that automatically responds to changes in line water pressure to maintain temperature; the valve blocks abrupt drop or rise in temperature.

Apron: The front extension of a bathtub that runs from the rim to the floor.

Awning window: A window with a single framed-glass panel. It is hinged at the top to swing out when it is open.

Backlighting: Illumination coming from a source behind or at the side of an object.

Backsplash: The finish material that covers the wall behind a countertop. The backsplash can be attached to the countertop or separate from it.

Barrier-free fixtures: Fixtures specifically designed for disabled individuals who use wheelchairs or who have limited mobility.

Baseboard: A trim board attached as part of a base treatment to the bottom of a wall where it meets the floor.

Base cabinet: A cabinet that rests on the floor under a countertop or vanity.

Base plan: A map of an existing bathroom that shows detailed measurements and the location of fixtures and their permanent elements.

Basin: A shallow sink.

Bidet: A bowl-shaped fixture that supplies water for personal hygiene. It looks similar to a toilet.

Blanket insulation: Flexible insulation, such as fiberglass or mineral wool, that comes packaged in long rolls.

Blocking: A small piece of wood used to reinforce framing members.

Bridging: Lumber or metal installed in an X shape between floor joists to stabilize and position the joists.

Built-in: A cabinet, shelf, medicine chest, or other storage unit that is recessed into the wall.

Bump out: Living space created by cantilevering the floor and ceiling joists (or adding to a floor slab) and extending the exterior wall of a room.

Cable: One or more wires enclosed in protective plastic or metal sheathing.

Candlepower (Cp): The intensity of light measured at the light source.

Cantilever: A structural beam supported on one end. A cantilever can be used to support a bump out.

Casement window: A window that consists of one framed-glass panel that is hinged on the side. It swings outward from the opening at the turn of a crank.

Casing: The general term for any trim that surrounds a window.

Cement-based backer board: A rigid panel designed for use as a substrate for ceramic tiles in wet areas.

Centerline: The dissecting line through the center of an object, such as a sink.

CFM: An abbreviation that refers to the amount of cubic feet of air that is moved per minute by an exhaust fan.

Chair rail: A decorative wall molding installed midway between the floor and ceiling. Traditionally, chair rails protected walls from damage from chair backs.

Cleanout: A removable plug in a trap or drainpipe, which allows easy access for removing blockages.

Clearance: The amount of space between two fixtures, the centerlines of two fixtures, or a fixture and an obstacle, such as a wall. Clearances may be mandated by building codes.

Cleat: A piece of lumber fastened—to a joist or post, for example—as a support for other lumber.

Closet bend: A curved section of drain beneath the base of a toilet.

Closet flange: The rim of a closet bend used to attach the toilet drainpipe to the floor.

Code: A locally or nationally enforced mandate regarding structural design, materials, plumbing, or electrical systems that states what you can or cannot do when you build or remodel. Codes are intended to protect standards of health, safety, and land use.

Color rendition index (CRI): Measures the way a light source renders color. The higher the index number, the closer colors illuminated by the light source resemble how they appear in sunlight.

Combing: A painting technique that involves using a small device with teeth or grooves over a wet painted surface to create a grained effect.

Contemporary style: A style of decoration or architecture that is modern and pertains to what is current.

Cornice: Any molding or group of moldings used in the corner between a wall and a ceiling.

Correlated color temperature (CCT): A value assigned to a fluorescent lamp indicating the warmth or coolness of the light it produces.

Countertop: The work surface of a counter, usually 36 inches high. Common countertop materials include stone, plastic laminate, ceramic tile, concrete, and solid surfacing.

Cove lights: Lights that reflect upward, sometimes located on top of wall cabinets.

Crown molding: A decorative molding usually installed where the wall and ceiling meet.

Dimmer switch: A switch that can vary the intensity of the light source that it controls.

Door casing: The trim applied to a wall around the edge of a door frame.

Double-glazed window: A window consisting of two panes of glass separated by a space that contains air or argon gas. The space provides most of the insulation.

glossary

Double-hung window: A window that consists of two framed-glass panels that slide open vertically, guided by a metal or wood track.

Downlighting: A lighting technique that illuminates objects or areas from above.

Duct: A tube or passage for venting indoor air to the outside.

Enclosure: Any material used to form a shower or tub stall, such as glass, glass block, or a tile wall.

Escutcheon: A decorative plate that covers a hole in the wall in which the pipe stem or cartridge fits.

Faux painting: Various painting techniques that mimic wood, marble, and other stones.

Fittings: The plumbing devices that transport water to the fixtures. These can include showerheads, faucets, and spouts. Also pertains to hardware and some accessories, such as towel racks, soap dishes, and toilet-paper dispensers.

Fixed window: A window that cannot be opened. It is usually a decorative unit, such as a half-round or Palladian-style window.

Fixture: Any fixed part of the structural design, such as tubs, bidets, toilets, and lavatories.

Fixture spacing: The amount of space

included between ambient light fixtures to achieve an even field of illumination in a given area.

Fluorescent lamp: An energy-efficient light source made of a tube with an interior phosphorus coating that glows when energized by electricity.

Flux: The material applied to the surface of copper pipes and fittings when soldering to assist in the cleaning and bonding process.

Foot-candle (Fc): A unit that is used to measure the brightness produced by a lamp. A foot-candle is equal to one lumen per square foot of surface.

Form: The shape and structure of space or an object.

Full bath: A bath that includes a toilet, lavatory, and bathing fixtures, such as a tub or shower.

Furring: Wood strips used to level parts of a ceiling, wall, or floor before adding the finish surface. Also used to secure panels of rigid insulation. Sometimes called strapping.

Glass blocks: Decorative building blocks made of translucent glass used for non-load-bearing walls to allow passage of light.

Glazing (walls): A technique for applying a thinned, tinted wash of translucent color to a dry undercoat of paint.

Ground-fault circuit interrupter (GFCI): A safety circuit breaker that compares the amount of current entering a receptacle with the amount leaving. If there is a discrepancy of 0.005 volt, the GFCI breaks the circuit in a fraction of a second. GFCIs are required by the National Electrical Code in areas of the house that are subject to dampness.

Grout: A binder and filler applied in the joints between ceramic tile.

Half bath (powder room): A bathroom that contains only a toilet and a sink.

Halogen bulb: A bulb filled with halogen gas, a substance that causes the particles of tungsten to be redeposited onto the tungsten filament. This process extends the lamp's life and makes the light whiter and brighter.

Hardboard: Manufactured pressed-wood panels; hardboard is rejected by some manufacturers as an acceptable substrate for resilient and tile floors.

Highlight: The lightest tone in a room.

Incandescent lamp: A bulb that contains a conductive filament through which current flows. The current reacts with an inert gas inside the bulb, which makes the filament glow.

Intensity: Strength of a color.

Jamb: The frame around a window or door.

Jets: Nozzles installed behind the walls of tubs or showers that pump out pressurized streams of water.

Joist: Set in a parallel fashion, these framing members support the boards of a ceiling or a floor.

Junction box: Electrical box in which all standard wiring splices and connections are made.

Lavatory or lav: A fixed bowl or basin with running water and a drainpipe that is used for washing.

Load-bearing wall: A wall that supports a structure's vertical load. Openings in any load-bearing wall must be reinforced to carry the live and dead weight of the structure's load.

Low-voltage lights: Lights that operate on 12 to 50 volts rather than the standard 120 volts.

Lumen: A term that refers to the intensity of light measured at a light source that is used for general or ambient lighting.

Medallion: A decorative, usually round relief, carving applied to a wall.

Molding: Decorative strips of wood or plastic used in various kinds of trimwork.

Muntins: Framing members of a window that divide the panes of glass.

Nonbearing wall: A wall that does not support the weight of areas above it.

On center: A point of reference for measuring. For example, 16 inches on center means 16 inches from the center of one framing member to the center of the next.

Overflow: An outlet positioned in a tub or sink that allows water to escape if a faucet is left open.

Palette: A range of colors that complement each other.

Pedestal: A stand-alone lavatory with a basin and supporting column in one piece.

Pilaster: A vertical relief molding attached to a wall, usually made to resemble the surface of a pillar.

Pocket door: A door that opens by sliding inside the wall, as opposed to a conventional door that opens into a room.

glossary

Pressure-balancing valve: Also known as a surge protector or antiscalding device. It is a control that prevents surges of hot or cold water in faucets by equalizing the amounts of hot and cold water pumped out at any time.

Proportion: The relationship of one object to another.

Radiant floor heat: A type of heating that is brought into a room via electrical wire or pipes (to carry hot water) that have been installed under the floor. As the pipes or electrical wire heats up, the flooring material warms and heat rises into the room.

Ragging: A painting technique that uses a crumbled piece of cloth to apply or remove small amounts of wet paint to create a pattern or texture.

Rail: Horizontal trimwork installed on a wall between the cornice and base trim. It may stand alone, as a chair rail, or be part of a larger framework.

Reflectance levels: The amount of light that is reflected from a colored surface, such as a tile wall or painted surface.

Resilient flooring: Thin floor coverings composed of materials such as vinyl, rubber, cork, or linoleum. Comes in a wide range of colors and patterns in both tile and sheet forms.

Rigid foam: Insulating boards composed of polystyrene or polyisocyanurate that may be foil backed. Rigid insulation offers the highest R-value per inch of thickness.

Roof window: A horizontal window that is installed on the roof. Roof windows are ventilating.

Roughing-in: The installation of the water-supply and DWV pipes before the fixtures are in place.

Rubber float: A flat, rubber-faced tool used to apply grout.

Scale: The size of a room or object.

Schematic: A detailed diagram of systems within a home.

Sconce: A decorative wall bracket, sometimes made of iron or glass, that shields a bulb.

Sight line: The natural line of sight the eye travels when looking into or around a room.

Sister joist: A reinforcing joist added to the side of a cut or damaged joist for additional support.

Skylight: A framed opening in the roof that admits sunlight into the house. It can be covered with either a flat glass panel or a plastic dome.

Sliding window: Similar to a double-hung window turned on its side. The glass panels slide horizontally.

Snap-in grilles: Ready-made rectangular and diamond-pattern grilles that snap into a window sash and create the look of a true divided-light window.

Soffit: A boxed-in area just below the ceiling and above the vanity.

Soil stack: The main vertical pipe in a house that carries waste to the sewer or septic lines.

Spa: An in-ground or aboveground tublike structure or vessel that is equipped with whirlpool jets.

Space reconfiguration: A design term that is used to describe the reallocation of interior space without adding on.

Sponging: A paint technique that uses a small sponge to apply or remove small amounts of wet paint to create a pattern or texture on a surface.

Spout: The tube or pipe from which water gushes out of a faucet.

Spud washer: The large rubber ring placed over the drain hole of a two-piece toilet. The tank is placed over the spud washer.

Stencil: A design cut out of plastic or cardboard. When paint is applied to the cut-out area, the design will be reproduced on a surface.

Stippling: A decorative paint technique that involves applying paint to a wall with a stiff bristle brush.

Stock cabinets: Cabinets that are in stock or available quickly when ordered from a retail outlet.

Stops: On doors, the trim on the jamb that keeps the door from swinging through; on windows, the trim that covers the inside face of the jamb.

Stud: The vertical member of a frame wall placed at both ends and usually every 16 inches on center. A stud provides structural framing and facilitates covering with drywall or plywood.

Subfloor: The flooring applied directly to the floor joists on top of which the finished floor rests.

Surround: The enclosure and area around a tub or shower. A surround may include steps and a platform, as well as the tub itself.

Switch loop: Installation in which a switch is at the end of a circuit with one incoming power cable, and the outgoing neutral wire becomes a hot wire to control a fixture.

Task lighting: Lighting designed to illuminate a particular task, such as shaving.

Thickset: A layer of mortar that is more than ½ inch thick and is used as a base for setting ceramic tile.

Thinset: Any cement-based or organic adhesive applied in a layer less than ½ inch thick that is used for setting tile.

Three-quarter bath: A bathroom that contains a toilet, sink, and shower.

Tone: The degree of lightness or darkness of a color.

Tongue-and-groove: Boards milled with a protruding tongue on one edge and a slot on the other for a tight fit on flooring and paneling.

Traditional style: A style of decoration or architecture (typically of the eighteenth and nineteenth centuries) that employs forms that have been repeated for generations without major changes.

Trap: A section of curved pipe that forms a seal against sewer gas when it is filled with water.

Tripwaste: A lever-controlled bathtub drain stopper.

Trompe l'oeil: French for "fool the eye." A paint technique that creates a photographically real illusion of space or objects.

True divided-light window: A window composed of multiple glass panes that are divided by and held together by muntins.

Universal design: Products and designs that are easy to use by people of all ages, heights, and varying physical abilities.

Vanity: The countertop and cabinet unit that supports a sink. The vanity is usually included in the bathroom for storage purposes. It may also be used as a dressing table.

Vapor retarder: A material used to prevent water vapor from moving from one area into another or into a building material.

Vent stack: The main vertical vent pipe in the DWV system.

Ventilation: The process of removing or supplying air to a certain space.

Watt: The unit of measurement of electrical power required or consumed by a fixture or appliance.

Wax ring: A wax seal between the base of a toilet and the closet flange that prevents leaking.

Whirlpool: A special tub that includes motorized jets behind the walls of the tub for water massages.

Window stool: The horizontal surface installed below the sash of a window, often called a windowsill.

Wire connector: A small cap used for twisting two or more wires together.

Xenon bulb: A bulb similar to a halogen bulb, except that it is filled with xenon gas and does not emit ultraviolet (UV) rays. In addition, it is cooler and more energy efficient.

index

index

index

photo credits

Note: DDL=www.davidduncanlivingston.com

page 1: courtesy of Armstrong **page 3:** Anne Gummerson, design: Julie and Ken Girardini **page 4:** Tria Giovan **pages 6–7:** *left and top right* DDL; *bottom right* courtesy of Kohler **pages 8–9:** Mark Lohman, architect: Bill Nicolas **pages 10–11:** *all* DDL **pages 12–13:** *all* Olson Photography, LLC, *left and center* design: Nina Cuccio Peck Architecture & Interiors; *right* design: Putnam Kitchens **pages 14–15:** *all* Olson Photography, LLC, design: Legacy Development Northeast LLC **pages 16–17:** *all* Olson Photography, LLC; *top* design: Amazing Spaces; *bottom* builder: Four Square Builders Inc. **pages 18–19:** Olson Photography, LLC, design: General Woodcraft **page 20:** Eric Roth, design: www.heidipribell.com **page 21:** Olson Photography, LLC, builder: Four Square Builders Inc. **page 22:** Eric Roth, *top* design: www.trikeenan.com; *bottom* DDL **page 23:** *top* Olson Photography, LLC, design: Sharon Cameron Lawn Interiors; *bottom right* DDL; *left* Eric Roth, design: www.TBAdesigns.com **page 25:** Olson Photography, LLC, design: CK Architects **pages 26–27:** Mark Samu, builder: Bonacio Construction **page 28:** Olson Photography, LLC, design: Design Build Collaborative **page 29:** Olson Photography, LLC, builder: Titus Built **page 31:** *all* Olson Photography, LLC; *right* architect: Paul Shainberg Architects; *left* architect: Studio Dumitru Architects **page 33:** *right* Eric Roth; *left* courtesy of Jaclo **pages 34–35:** Eric Roth, design: www.lesliefineinte-riors.com **page 36:** *top* DDL; *bottom* Tria Giovan **page 37:** *top* Bill Rothschild; *bottom* DDL **page 38:** Eric Roth, design: www.svdesign.com **page 39:** *top* Eric Roth; *bottom right* Tria Giovan; *bottom left* DDL **page 40:** *top* DDL; *bottom* courtesy of Neptune **page 41:** *all* courtesy of Neptune **pages 42–43:** *top right* courtesy of Neptune; *bottom center* DDL; *bottom left* Tria Giovan; *bottom right* courtesy of Neptune **page 44:** *top* Anne Gummerson, design: Shelly Curry, Architect, Raphael Homes Builder; *bottom* Mark Samu, design: Lucianna Samu Design **page 45:** *top* courtesy of Wetstyle; *bottom* Anne Gummerson, architect: Andre Fontaine **page 46:** *all* DDL **page 47:** *top* courtesy of The McCoy Group; *bottom* courtesy of Neptune **pages 48–49:** *top right* Mark Samu, design: Donald Billinkoff, AIA; *bottom right* Mark Samu, design: Kollath-McCann

Design; *left* Eric Roth, design: www.brittadesign.com **page 50:** *left* Eric Roth, design: www.trikeenan.com; *top right* DDL; *bottom right* courtesy of Price Pfister **page 51:** *top* DDL; *bottom* Mark Samu, design: SD Atelier AIA **page 52:** *top left* courtesy of Jaclo Showers; *top right and center* Mark Lohman, design: Janet Lohman & Anne Leeds; *bottom left* courtesy of Kohler **page 53:** courtesy of Jaclo Showers **page 54:** *top* Eric Roth, design: www.brittadesign.com; *bottom* courtesy of REHAU **page 55:** *top* Mark Lohman; *bottom* courtesy of Jaclo Showers **pages 56–57:** Bill Rothschild **pages 58–59:** *top center* DDL; *top right* Olson Photography, LLC, design: Legacy Development Northeast LLC; *bottom left to right* Tony Giammarino/GiammarinoDworkin; Olson Photography, LLC, design: Kitchen & Bath Designs by Betsy House; DDL; Mark Lohman, design: Roxanne Packham Design **page 60:** Mark Lohman, design: Sue McKeehan **page 61:** *top* Eric Roth, design: www.designlabarch.com; *bottom* Mark Lohman, design: William Hefner **pages 62–63:** *top left* Tria Giovan; *top center* Mark Lohman, design: Kathryne Design; *top right* Eric Roth, design: www.trike-enan.com; *bottom right* Mark Samu, design: Lucianna Samu Design; *bottom left* Olson Photography, LLC, design: Sally Scott Interiors **page 64:** *top left* Mark Lohman, design: Maraya Droney Design; *top right* Mark Samu; *bottom* Mark Samu, architect: Bokor Architecture **page 65:** *top* Olson Photography, LLC, design: Brindisi & Yaroscak; *bottom* DDL **pages 66–67:** *top center* Olson Photography, LLC, builder: Four Square Builders Inc.; *bottom center* Mark Samu, builder: Bonacio Construction; *right* Olson Photography, LLC, design: Kitchen & Bath Designs by Betsy House **pages 68–69:** *left and center* Mark Samu, design: Jeanne Ziering Design; *top right* Eric Roth, design: www.gleysteendesign.com; *bottom right* Mark Samu, architect: Joe Vilardo **pages 70–71:** *top left to right* Tria Giovan; Mark Samu, architect: Bokor Architecture; Eric Roth, design: www.sternmccafferty.com; *bottom* Olson Photography, LLC, builder: Nobile Construction **page 72:** *top* Olson Photography, LLC, design: Brindisi & Yaroscak; *bottom* DDL; *right* courtesy of Sonoma Cast Stone **page 73:** Sergio Fama, courtesy of Art & Maison, Inc. **pages**

74–75: *top left* Lou Ann Bauer, ASID, Bauer Design; *top right, bottom left and center* courtesy of Sonoma Cast Stone; *bottom right* Sergio Fama, courtesy of Art & Maison, Inc. **page 76:** *top* courtesy of Corian; *bottom right* courtesy of Armstrong; *bottom left* Mark Samu, design: Todd Stewart Construction **page 77:** *top* courtesy of Corian; *bottom* courtesy of Armstrong **page 78:** Mark Lohman, design: Maraya Droney **page 79:** *top* courtesy of CaesarStone; *bottom right* courtesy of Zodiaq; *bottom left* courtesy of Wilsonart **page 80:** *all* courtesy of Wilsonart **page 81:** Olson Photography, LLC, design: Ambiente/Venlo **pages 82–83:** *top and bottom left* DDL; *bottom right* Mark Samu, design: Lucianna Samu Design **page 84:** *left* Beth Singer; *right* Mark Samu, design: Lucianna Samu Design **page 85:** Olson Photography, LLC, design: Brindisi & Yaroscak **pages 86–87:** Mark Lohman, design: Palm Design Group **pages 88–89:** *top left to right* courtesy of Kohler; courtesy of Hearst Magazines; Mark Lohman, design: Kyser Interiors; Mark Lohman; *bottom right* courtesy of Alchemy Glass; *bottom left* Mark Samu, design: Benvenuti & Stein **pages 90–91:** *clockwise* Olson Photography, LLC, design: Eric Strachan Custom Homes; Olson Photography, LLC, design: Olga Adler Interiors; DDL; Olson Photography, LLC, design: McWilliam-Autore Interiors; Olson Photography, LLC, builder: VAS Construction; Olson Photography, LLC, builder: Hemingway Construction; Olson Photography, LLC, builder: Hemingway Construction **pages 92–93:** *top left and center* Mark Lohman, design: Barclay Butera; *left* DDL; *bottom left* Mark Lohman, design: Nancy McDonald **page 94:** *top left* DDL; *top right* Eric Roth, design: www.weenaandspook.com; *bottom* Mark Lohman, design: Stephanie Hermelee **page 95:** *top* courtesy of Stone Forest; *bottom* courtesy of Alchemy Glass **pages 96–97:** *clockwise* Anne Gummerson; courtesy of Kohler; courtesy of Moen; DDL; Anne Gummerson, design: Julie and Ken Girardini **page 98:** *all* courtesy of Kohler **page 99:** *top* courtesy of Moen; *bottom* Mark Samu, design: Charles Reilly Design **page 100:** *top left and right* courtesy of Kohler; *bottom* courtesy of Moen **page 101:** *top left and right* courtesy of Moen; *bottom* courtesy of Kohler **pages 102–103:** *top and bottom left* courtesy of Toto; *top right* courtesy of Neo-Metro; *bottom* courtesy of Herbeau **page 104:** *left* Tony Giammarino/ Giammarino-Dworkin; *right* Mark Samu, design: Lucianna Samu Design **page 105:** *top* courtesy of Toto; *bottom* courtesy of Kohler **page 106:** *top* DDL; *bottom all* courtesy of Moen **page 107:** *top* courtesy of Kohler; *bottom all* courtesy Neo-Metro **page 108:** *top all* courtesy of Neo-Metro; *bottom* courtesy of Kohler **page 109:** *top* courtesy of Kohler; *bottom left and center* courtesy of Neo-Metro; *bottom right* courtesy of Neo-Metro **pages 110–111:** *left* courtesy of Kohler; *center* courtesy of Bemis; *top right and bottom* Mark Samu, design: Lucianna Samu Design **pages 112–113:** DDL **pages 114–115: pages 114–115:** *left* DDL; *top* Mark Lohman, design: Nancy McDonald; *bottom center* Mark Samu, architect: Bokor Architecture; *bottom right* Eric Roth design: www.pappasmiron.com **page 116:** *left* Olson Photography, LLC, architect: Peter Cadoux Architects; *right* Eric Roth, design: www.decoridesigns.com **page 117:** Anne Gummerson, design: Dan Proctor, Kirk Design **page 118:** *all* DDL **page 119:** Olson Photography, LLC, architect: White Architects **page 120:** *all* Olson Photography, LLC; *left* builder: Greenwich Home Builders; *right* design: Kitchen & Bath Designs by Betsy House **page 121:** *top* Eric Roth, design: www.brittadesign.com; *bottom* Olson Photography, LLC, architect: Peter Cadoux Architects **page 122:** *top and bottom left* DDL; *bottom right* Olson Photography, LLC, design: Total Design Source **page 123:** *top* Olson Photography, LLC, design: Northeast Cabinet Design; *bottom all* courtesy of Kraftmaid **pages 124–125:** *all* Anne Gummerson; *left* design: Julie and Ken Girardini; *right* design: Diane Altieri, Diane Designs and Associate **page 126:** Eric Roth, builder: www.fbnconstruction.net **page 127:** *all* Olson Photography, LLC; *top left* architect: Peter Cadoux Architects; *bottom left* builder: Titus Built; *left* design: Putnam Kitchens **page 128:** Olson Photography, LLC, builder: Stevenson Lumber **page 129:** Olson Photography, LLC, design: Jack Rosen Custom Kitchens **pages 130–131:** *all* courtesy of Merillat **page 132:** *left* Mark Samu, design: Donald Billinkoff AIA; *right* Olson Photography, LLC, design: J Interiors **page 133:** Olson Photography, LLC, architect: Elm City Architects **pages 134–135:** *top left and right* courtesy of Kraftmaid; *top center, bottom center and bottom left all* courtesy of Meril-

lat **page 136:** *top* Olson Photography, LLC, design: Cole Harris Associates; *bottom left* Olson Photography, LLC, builder: Nobile Construction; *bottom right* Mark Lohman, design: Sue McKeehan **page 137:** Anne Gummerson, design: Dan Proctor, Kirk Design **page 138:** *top* Mark Samu, design: Lucianna Samu Design; *bottom* Olson Photography, LLC, design: Joe Currie of Jack Rosen Custom Kitchens **page 139:** Olson Photography, LLC **pages 140–143:** *all* courtesy of Kohler **pages 144–149:** *all* Tria Giovan **page 150:** Anne Gummerson, design: Gina Fitzsimmons, Fitsimmons Design Associates **page 151:** *left* Mark Lohman, design: Will McGaul & Co.; *right* courtesy of Velux America **page 152:** *top* Olson Photography, LLC, design: Sharon McCormick Interiors; *bottom left* Anne Gummerson, design: Julie and Ken Girardini; *bottom right* Mark Samu, design: Donald Billinkoff AIA **page 153:** Olson Photography, LLC, design: Nancy Budd Interiors **pages 154–155:** *top left* Olson Photography, LLC, design: Brindisi & Yaroscak; *top center* Olson Photography, LLC, design: Kitchen & Bath Designs by Betsy House; *right* Eric Roth, design: www.heidipribell.com; *bottom center* Olson Photography, LLC, design: Sheridan Interiors **page 156:** *top* Olson Photography, LLC, builder: Avon Ridge Builders and Developers; *bottom left* Olson Photography, LLC, design: Olga Adler Interiors; *bottom right* Mark Lohman, design: Overmire & Assoc. **page 157:** *top* courtesy of Kohler; *bottom* Olson Photography, LLC, builder: Hemingway Construction **page 158:** *top left* Olson Photography, LLC, design: KLM Interiors; *top right* Olson Photography, LLC, builder: P&H Construction; *bottom* Eric Roth **page 159:** Mark Samu, design: The Michaels Group **pages 160–161:** *top left* Mark Lohman, design: Barclay Butera; *bottom left* courtesy of Artemide; *right* Eric Roth **page 162:** Mark Samu, builder: D. Reis Construction **page 163:** *top* courtesy of Kohler; *bottom* DDL **pages 164–165:** *left* Mark Samu, architect: Bokor Architecture; *center and bottom right* courtesy of Sea Gull Lighting; *top right* courtesy of Kohler **pages 166–167:** *left* Mark Lohman, design: Janet Lohman & Anne Leeds; *center* Olson Photography, LLC, design: Frank J. Mairano & Associates; *right* Olson Photography, LLC, architect: Sellars Lathrop Architects **pages 168–169:** *left* courtesy of NuTone; *right* Olson Photog-

raphy, LLC, architect: Peter Cadoux Architects **pages 170–171:** Olson Photography, LLC, architect: Paul Shainberg Architects **pages 172–173:** *top left and right* Olson Photography, LLC, architect: CK Architects; *bottom right* Eric Roth; *bottom left and center* Olson Photography, LLC, builder: Nobile Construction **page 174:** Olson Photography, LLC, builder: Greenwich Home Builders **page 175:** Mark Samu, design: Kollath-McCann Design **pages 176–177:** *left* Mark Lohman; *center* Olson Photography, LLC, design: Sharon McCormick Interiors; Olson Photography, LLC, design: Fieber Group **page 178:** Tony Giammarino/Giammarino-Dworkin **page 179:** *all* Olson Photography, LLC; *left* architect: Peter Cadoux Architects **page 180:** Mark Samu, builder: Amedore Construction **page 181:** *left* Mark Samu; *right* Tony Giammarino/GiammarinoDworkin; *bottom* Mark Samu, design: Artistic Designs by Deidre **pages 182-183:** *all* Olson Photography, LLC; *left* design: Olga Adler Interiors; *right* architect: Peter Cadoux Architects **page 184:** *all* Olson Photography, LLC; *top* design: Prime Homes; *bottom* design: Eric Strachan Custom Homes **page 185:** Bob Greenspan **page 187:** *top left* Nancy Elizabeth Hill; *top right* DDL; *bottom* Anne Gummerson **pages 188-189:** *left* Anne Gummerson, design: Arlene Dvorine, Interior Design; *right* Olson Photography, LLC, design: Caulfield & Ridgway, Inc. **pages 190-191:** *left* Tria Giovan; *top center* Mark Lohman, design: Sue McKeehan; *right* Olson Photography, LLC, design: Nest of Southport; *bottom center* Anne Gummerson, architect: Alt Breeding Schwarz **page 192:** *top* Anne Gummerson, builder: Post and Beam Design-Build; *bottom* Tria Giovan **page 193:** *top* Tony Giammarino/Giammarino-Dworkin; *bottom* Anne Gummerson, design: Julie and Ken Girardini **pages 194-195:** *all* DDL **pages 196-197:** *all* Tony Giammarino/GiammarinoDworkin **pages 198-199:** *all* DDL **pages 200-201:** *all* Bob Greenspan **page 202:** Mark Lohman, design: Roxanne Packham Design **page 203:** *all* Roger Wade **page 205:** Mark Samu, design: SD Atelier AIA **page 206:** Anne Gummerson, design: Gina Fitzsimmons, Fitsimmons Design Associates **page 211:** Bill Rothschild **page 212:** Mark Samu, architect: Bokor Architecture **page 217:** Anne Gummerson, design: Dan Proctor, Kirk Design **page 221:** Eric Roth, design: www.brittadesign.com

If you like
Design Ideas For Bathrooms,
take a look at these and other books in the
Design Ideas Series.

Design Ideas for Kitchens
Design inspiration for creating a new and improved kitchen. Over 500 photos.
224 pp.; 8½" x 10⅞"
BOOK #279412

REVISED AND EXPANDED

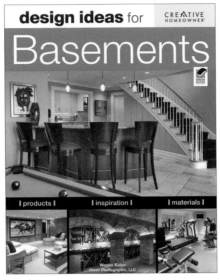

Design Ideas for Basements
Design solutions for putting your basement space to good use. Over 300 color photos. 208 pp.; 8½" x 10⅞"
BOOK #279424

Design Ideas for Decks & Patios
Design inspiration for creating the deck or patio of your dreams. Over 260 photos.
224 pp.; 8½" x 10⅞"
BOOK #279534

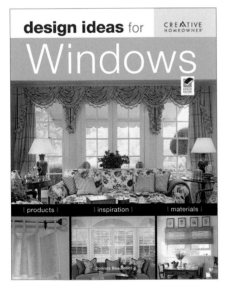

Design Ideas for Windows
Hundreds of window treatments and ideas for every room. Over 400 photos.
256 pp.; 8½" x 10⅞"
BOOK #279376

Design Ideas for Home Decorating
Design solutions for every room, on every budget. Over 500 photos.
320 pp.; 8½" x 10⅞"
BOOK #279323

Design Ideas for Home Landscaping
Inspiring ideas to achieve stunning effects with landscape. Over 350 photos.
240 pp; 8½" x 10⅞"
BOOK #274154

For more information and to order direct, go to **www.creativehomeowner.com**